CHURCHILL

THE GREATEST BRITON
IN WORDS, PICTURES AND RARE DOCUMENTS
FROM HIS OFFICIAL ARCHIVE

CHRISTOPHER CATHERWOOD

ANDRE
DEUTSCH

£2·99

THIS IS AN ANDRÉ DEUTSCH BOOK

Text © Christopher Catherwood 2012
Design © André Deutsch 2018

Quotations from Winston S. Churchill permission of Curtis Brown Ltd, London on behalf
of The Estate of Sir Winston Churchill, copyright © Winston S. Churchill

Published in association with Churchill Heritage Ltd. Churchill Heritage works in association
with the Churchill family and Estate of Sir Winston Churchill to support charities and good
causes associated with preserving the heritage and legacy of Sir Winston Churchill.

This edition published in 2018 by Andre Deutsch
A division of the Carlton Publishing Group
20 Mortimer Street
London
W1T 3JW

The content of this book first appeared in *Churchill: The Treasures of Winston Churchill, the
Greatest Briton* in 2012, ISBN: 978 0 233 00363 4.

Printed in Dubai

A CIP catalogue for this book is available from the British Library

ISBN: 978 0 233 00537 9

Contents

Introduction

Winston Churchill was voted the greatest Briton of all time in an extensive opinion poll, one taken many years after his death, with many of the voters not even alive during his lifetime.

In the second decade of the twenty-first century he remains as iconic a figure as ever, as much in the United States, his mother's home country, as in his own, with news coming of a new centre for the study of his achievements to be based in Washington DC, a city he came to know well during his many visits to the Roosevelt White House during the Second World War.

Does he still justify that status, as the Golden Jubilee of his passing comes upon us? I think that the answer surely remains "yes", even more because we can now see him in perspective in a way that was impossible while he was still alive. He was not perfect, and he certainly made mistakes that this book does not ignore. But the defence of Britain in 1940 against the Nazi menace was not just the struggle of two nations but of two radically different ways of looking at the world, of freedom, liberty, justice and democracy on the one side and tyranny, racism, mass murder and conquest on the other. This was something that Churchill, with his abiding love of history and of moral certainties understood so well. In defending us from Hitler he was protecting civilization itself.

Some of what follows will be familiar. Other parts of his life might be new to many readers, and either way the sheer scale of Churchill's unique life never loses its spell. The illustrations and memorabilia in this book will enable us to commemorate Churchill in an especially appealing way, a treasure itself of Churchill's treasures.

Christopher Catherwood

1

YOUNG WINSTON

The Churchills

Winston Churchill was born in Blenheim Palace, one of the largest and grandest palaces in Europe, and possibly the biggest outside royal ownership. It was a gift to his ancestor John Churchill, 1st Duke of Marlborough, by a grateful sovereign Queen Anne. It is the seat of the current duke to this day.

John Churchill (1650–1722) was the son of politician and minor landowner Sir Winston Churchill, and grandson of Sarah Winston (from whom came the famous first name). His family had been Cavaliers in the English Civil War, and had been financially punished by the government of the Commonwealth and Protectorate.

John Churchill became a mix of soldier and young courtier on the make: the best way for an ambitious man without fortune to rise above genteel poverty. Through his links with James, Duke of York (later King James II) – whose sometime mistress was John's sister Arabella – he rose in the ranks, and in 1685 he helped to crush a rebellion by Charles II's illegitimate son the Duke of Monmouth, thereby ensuring James II's succession to the throne. But in 1688, when a rebellion by the Whig faction in Parliament led to a potential civil war, Churchill switched sides. Supporting the rebels, he ended up on the right side of what history now calls the Glorious Revolution which ended the threat of monarchical dictatorship by a Stuart king.

John Churchill was also fortunate in his marriage to Sarah Jennings (1660–1744). This was a rare love match, and his wife was for a time the court favourite of James's younger daughter Queen Anne (reigned 1702–14). As a female monarch, Anne could not command the troops in battle, but, fortunately for Britain and its Continental allies against King Louis XIV of France, in Churchill the allied forces had a victory-winning captain-general. His most famous victory against France was the Battle of Blenheim (in Germany) in 1704, with others at Ramillies, Oudenarde and Malplaquet following later. In 1711, Churchill was dismissed from office due to court intrigue, but with the accession of the Hanoverian King George I in 1714, he was restored to favour and his reputation as one of Britain's greatest-ever commanders, along with the Duke of Wellington against Napoleon, was secure.

No one was more proud of an illustrious ancestor than Winston Churchill, whose multi-volume life of the Duke of Marlborough (as John Churchill became in 1702) was long the definitive treatment. And John's strategy and tactics against King Louis XIV deeply influenced Winston's own thinking about how to fight Hitler more than 200 years later.

RIGHT: Winston Churchill's illustrious ancestor, the great commander John Churchill, 1st Duke of Marlborough.

Blenheim Palace _____

Blenheim is vast: the building alone covers three hectares (seven acres). The estate at Woodstock, 12 kilometres (seven miles) from Oxford, was originally royal: Henry II's mistress "Fair Rosamund" lived there. It was given by Queen Anne to the new Duke and Duchess of Marlborough as a reward for the victory of Blenheim in 1704, hence the name. But the Churchills were far from rich and when John Churchill fell temporarily out of favour, they found the upkeep often beyond their means – slender finances would dog the family right down to their famous descendant.

Churchill's "Black Dog" ___

Ever since the seventeenth century, there had been a strong strain of emotional frailty in the Churchill family: Winston was to prove no exception. He called his version of depression his "black dog", as good a description as any. At that time, mental illness was not understood or easily treatable with medication, and even in our own twenty-first century it is unusual for public figures to admit to any kind of depression. So for one of the great icons of twentieth-century history to be outed as a sufferer is still controversial, especially given Churchill's other image, that of the indefatigable British bulldog.

When Churchill died, psychiatrists such as Anthony Storr probed further, examining his egotism and his occasional infantile, petulant behaviour. More recently the historian Richard Holmes speculated about the possibility of Asperger's Syndrome, in relation to the way in which Churchill treated his colleagues.

The detailed diaries of his physician Lord Moran show clearly that Churchill's "black dog" was a very straightforward – and nowadays largely treatable – form of depression, inherited from his illustrious Marlborough ancestors, and also shown in his later dependence upon alcohol. As for what else Churchill suffered from, we can only speculate, but we can conclude with three key reflections. First, for a man who suffered from depression, his tremendous achievements are all the more amazing, for in keeping going – especially in 1940 – he had much to overcome to be able to lead in the way he did. Second, Churchill used proper therapeutic behaviour, such as learning to paint, to help overcome his darkest days. And last, as many have pointed out, most rational people would have given up in 1940 with Britain's plight beyond desperate: Churchill, with his romantic view of "our Island story", persisted against all the odds.

LEFT: *The Battle of Blenheim* in 1704, with Churchill's famous ancestor commanding the coalition forces that beat the French. Painting by John Wootton, 1743.

Early Years

Winston Leonard Spencer Churchill was born on 30 November 1874. Like many aristocrats of his time, he had Anglo-American ancestry. His father, Lord Randolph Churchill, was the younger son of the 7th Duke of Marlborough. His American mother was born Jennie Jerome, daughter of Wall Street financier Leonard Jerome.

Unlike the arranged match of his brother to a Vanderbilt heiress, however, Lord Randolph's marriage was for love not money, as his father-in-law had lost as well as made several fortunes. (Significantly, the young Winston's lack of hereditary wealth to match his status was to later compel him to find work in a way that few of his class were obliged to do.)

Churchill's childhood – as vividly portrayed in his bestselling book *My Early Life* – was famously unhappy. In this he was not alone among the British upper and professional classes – C S Lewis was equally miserable, for example – but the difference is that with Churchill we know about his torment because he describes it so winsomely. He adored his parents, both of whom ignored him – again not a rare occurrence in such circles – and in the letters he wrote to them pleading for attention (wonderfully collected in his granddaughter Celia Sandys's book *From Winston With Love and Kisses*) one easily feels his isolation and sense of rejection.

Lord Randolph was a Conservative politician, sitting in the House of Commons for the Churchill-dominated borough of Woodstock which encompassed Blenheim. He was perceived as brilliant, an outstanding orator, but also as someone notoriously lacking in judgment and prone to attack his own side as much as dutifully supporting it. This maverick reputation got him noticed, and also did him no good with more orthodox politicians such as his party leader, the eminent Tory statesman Lord Salisbury, whose total of 13 years as Prime Minister has not been surpassed since.

Jennie, or Lady Randolph, as she was formally known, was a major society beauty of her time, someone who did not escape the notice of the Prince of Wales (later Edward VII). Churchill's parents cut a very considerable dash, which sadly meant that they had precious little time for their devoted and psychologically very needy small son. Psychiatrists have made much of this ever since.

However, Churchill, like many lonely children of his class, was saved by a devoted nanny, Mrs (Elizabeth) Everest, who, until her death in 1895, was to give him all the substitute maternal love he craved. He called her "Womany" and, although he did not always behave himself and was a fairly uncontrollable child,

she compensated for a great deal of his rejection.

After a series of unhappy boarding schools, Winston was sent in April 1888 to the famous Harrow School – unlike many Conservative leaders Churchill was not an Old Etonian. His time at Harrow was not academically successful, to the despair of the headmaster, Dr Welldon, who nevertheless realized Churchill possessed "some great gifts". The young Winston's love of oratory began at Harrow, where he wrote of his English class: "I got into my bones the essential structure of the ordinary British sentence – which is a noble thing."

His parents continued to be highly neglectful, even though Lord Randolph was no longer in office after the implosion of his meteoric political career in late 1886, when he resigned over-hastily as Chancellor of the Exchequer, never to hold office again. As Winston wrote in sorrow to them in 1889 to persuade them to come to Speech Day: "I do hope that both you & Mamma will come as last Speech Day nobody came to see me & it was very dull. You have never been to see me & so everything will be new to you... PS: I shall be awfully disappointed if you don't come..."

Years later one can still feel his pain...

And even at the end of his time in Harrow, in 1891, when he was in trouble for misbehaviour (he was beaten by the headmaster) and trying to enter Sandhurst, we find him writing to his mother: "Why have you not written to me, as you said you would, in answer to my 3 letters! I think it is very unkind of you..."

Churchill's granddaughter Celia Sandys makes an interesting point: Jennie Churchill was an American – how many British

OPPOSITE TOP: Winston with his mother (née Jennie Jerome) and his younger brother John, in 1886.

OPPOSITE LEFT: Winston Churchill as a four-year-old – with ringlets. Painting by Aryon War, 1878.

OPPOSITE RIGHT: Lord Randolph Churchill, Winston's emotionally absent father.

aristocratic mothers would have even allowed such a correspondence with their sons?

Then in 1893 he gained a place at Sandhurst, and his military career, which would soon propel him to national fame, began.

Lord Randoph Churchill's relations with his son never prospered. As Winston lamented after Lord Randolph died in 1895: "[If] ever I began to show the slightest idea of comradeship he was immediately offended; and when I once suggested that I might help... he froze me into stone."

It was a tragic legacy from which his son would never fully recover.

LEFT: Winston as a Harrow schoolboy in 1889: he was unhappy at the school, but gained a thorough education in history and the classics.

BELOW: Winston in fancy dress as a clown just before going to Harrow.

Churchill.

S. GEORGE'S SCHOOL,
ASCOT.

Report from *March 1st* to *April 9th 1884*

Place in School Order in Division at the end of last Term.	5th	Present place in New School order for Term.	6th

<table>
<tr><td rowspan="7">Division Master's Classical Report.</td><td colspan="2">Place in 4   Division of 11   Boys for Term.   6th</td></tr>
<tr><td>Composition</td><td>Improved.</td></tr>
<tr><td>Translation</td><td>Improved.</td></tr>
<tr><td>Grammar</td><td>Improved.</td></tr>
<tr><td>Diligence</td><td>Conduct has been exceedingly bad. He is not to be trusted to do any one thing. He has however notwithstanding made decided progress. —</td></tr>
<tr><td>No. of times late</td><td>20. very disgraceful.   Very bad. H.W.S.K.</td></tr>
</table>

<table>
<tr><td rowspan="4">Set Master's Report.</td><td colspan="2">Place in 4th   Set of 11   Boys for Term   6th</td></tr>
<tr><td>Mathematics</td><td>Improved.</td></tr>
<tr><td>French</td><td>Improved.</td></tr>
<tr><td>German</td><td>~</td></tr>
</table>

Scripture	Pass 60 out of 120. f
History	} very good, especially History. —
Geography	
Writing and Spelling	Both very much improved. —
Music	Promising.
Drawing	fair, considering. H. Martin Cooke.
General Conduct	Very bad — is a constant trouble to everybody, and is always in some scrape or other.
Headmaster's Remarks	He cannot be trusted to behave himself anywhere — He has very good abilities

Head Master.

H W Sneyd Kynnersley.

Winston Churchill was famously unhappy and out of control at school, as one glimpse of this sad school report makes vividly clear. He was either "very bad" or "exceedingly bad" and was certainly no scholar, except, significantly for the future, at history. Churchill is surely living proof that a bad start does not entail a poor finish.

The Adventurer

Winston Churchill was renowned for his bravery, having established this reputation early on in his life. We know about it because of another of his many gifts, that of writing. Many young soldiers of his era would have had adventures and tales of derring-do to relate to their admiring friends and family; in Churchill's case these tales are widely known because he transformed them into page-turning books which are still read today.

No famous university can claim Churchill as a graduate: the Royal Military Academy of Sandhurst has that honour. We associate Churchill with martial values, yet he also demonstrated himself to be a fine sportsman while an officer cadet there. He was a superb horseman – cavalry officers were to be predominantly horsebacked until the 1940s – and he became an expert polo player, a sport that he would continue to play well into his fifties. He even took up horseracing, riding in the 4th Hussars Subalterns' Cup, and altogether he frequently spent as many as eight hours a day in the saddle. Besides equestrianism, he became an expert rifleman, and took up fencing. Considering how unhealthy he had been as a child, this was a major turnaround for him. As his biographer Geoffrey Best has suggested, the sense of élan for mounted cavalry that Churchill developed as an officer cadet never left him. His love of taking the military offensive that marked his time in war in both 1914–18 and, especially, after 1940, is proof that he remained a cavalryman at heart.

Churchill was commissioned into one of the smarter cavalry regiments, the 4th Hussars, graduating from Sandhurst a very creditable twentieth out of a total of 130 new officers. He was also now head of his family, his father having died on 24 January 1895. If Churchill was never to be a conventional politician, he was certainly not an average soldier either. Not for him was the slow progress up the chain of regimental command – rather than kill time waiting for the Hussars to transfer to India, he and a fellow officer decided to find a war for themselves.

This was in Cuba, then in the process of trying to gain independence from Spain. After gaining a journalistic commission to report the war for *The Daily Graphic*, Churchill left for Havana, thus beginning his alternative career as a writer that was to sustain him financially when out of political office for much of the rest of his life. While not in Cuba for long, he had his first taste of being under enemy fire on his twenty-first birthday, when the Spanish column to which he was attached came under rebel attack.

He soon found himself on regular garrison duty in Bangalore, southern India, with the 4th Hussars. This he found boring and restrictive, but he set himself the task of reading as much as possible

– including the great literary historians such as Edward Gibbon and Thomas Babington Macaulay – while not forgetting to play polo with his less cerebral colleagues.

However, the heat and boredom soon got the better of him. In April 1897, he heard that General Sir Bindon Blood was setting up an expedition to crush rebellious Pathans in the legendary Northwest Frontier region of the Raj. (Pathans are now called Pashtuns, and that area is now the Taliban-infested border zone between Pakistan and Afghanistan.) The expedition was named the Malakand Field Force, and, after pulling as many strings as possible, Churchill enlisted on it not just as an officer but also as a war correspondent for *The Daily Telegraph*.

As in the twenty-first century, the Pathans were a dangerous enemy. In one skirmish in the Mamund valley, Churchill found himself in considerable peril though he emerged unscathed. His adventures were soon published as his first book, *The Story of the Malakand Field Force*, which was glowingly reviewed and helped to put its youthful author on the map. However, senior officers took less sanguine a view – Churchill had been very honest about the expedition's failures as well as its successes, and since he was a distinctly junior subaltern his reports were seen as deeply impertinent.

Churchill had hoped to go on another campaign, but this time his aspirations were thwarted. He instead completed a novel, *Savrola*, whose lack of success made it his only foray into fiction. However, another and even more exciting war now beckoned: in the Sudan. The British hero General Charles Gordon "of Khartoum" had been murdered by the rebel forces of the Mahdi, an Islamic warrior/prophet, in 1885, and now, in 1898, the British – under their leading army commander General Sir Herbert Kitchener – launched an expedition of revenge and reconquest.

OPPOSITE: Churchill (left) in 1894 at Sandhurst with two fellow officer cadets.

TOP LEFT: Churchill in khaki service dress in Bangalore in 1897, where pastimes included playing polo. His experiences in India helped to launch his literary career.

TOP RIGHT: Churchill in 1895, wearing his regimental uniform as a lieutenant of the 4th Queen's Own Hussars.

The young and enthusiastic Churchill did everything possible to get to the Sudan. Kitchener was doubtful about him, but Churchill's loyal mother was able to pull strings and he was attached to the expedition both as an officer in the 21st Lancers and also as a reporter for *The Morning Post*. So it was that on 2 September 1898, Churchill and the British army found themselves at Omdurman in the Sudan, facing – as Churchill was later to put it – "forty thousand hostile spear points". When battle commenced, the 21st Lancers engaged and defeated several thousand Dervish warriors in what became the last-ever major cavalry charge in the history of the British army. Once again Churchill wrote about his experiences in a bestselling book, *The River War*.

But now his ultimate goal – politics – beckoned. In the summer of 1899, there was a by-election in the Lancashire mill town of Oldham, and he raced back from Africa to contest the seat as a Conservative. Despite his efforts, he lost, the future leader's first attempt to enter the political world knocked back.

However, Churchill was once more summoned by the sound of gunfire. By October 1899, the British were at war in another part of Africa and Winston was off on his adventures again…

ABOVE: An 1899 painting entitled *The Charge of the 21st Lancers at the Battle of Omdurman on 2 September 1898*, by Edward Matthew Hale.

No.   Date

From *Lieut Churchill*

Place   Des^p *6* h. *30* m. M

To *Sirdar*

Place   Rec^d h. m. M

About 1/4 Dervish army is on their right which they have reposed at present.

Should their force continue to advance it would come the South side of Heliograph hill.

Most of the cavalry are with this force.

———

Duplicate to Col. Martin

Signature *Winston S. Churchill*
       Lieut 4th Hussars

The Battle of Omdurman was one of the last great cavalry charges in the proud history of British cavalry, and as his despatch shows, Churchill played a brave and active role in charging against the "Dervish" horsemen as part of Kitchener's victory over the Mahdi in Sudan.

Prisoner of the Boers

Churchill was a man who wanted to be where the action was – and in late 1899, that was South Africa, where the Second Boer War had broken out. Britain was fighting against the breakaway Boer (Dutch-origin) Orange Free State and South African Republic (Transvaal). It was a conflict with ups and downs for the British, and controversial for their use of "concentration camps", whereby Boer civilians were herded into concentrated areas, with unintended and devastating effects, including thousands of deaths.

Churchill first had to resign his commission, since he could initially only go to South Africa as a civilian – something that was very quickly to prove a godsend. As always, he was able to pull strings. He got himself accredited as the special correspondent of the newspaper *The Morning Post* and, through his father's old friend Joseph Chamberlain (the Colonial Secretary and father of Neville), gained many useful introductions for when he arrived. Churchill was already a war hero and his book on the Sudan, *The River War*, a major seller. And by pure luck, the ship on which he travelled out there, the *Dunottar Castle*, was also carrying the British commander in chief, Sir Redvers Buller.

Typically, on arrival Churchill set off to observe the thick of the fighting as soon as possible. He met up with a friend from his India days, Captain Aylmer Haldane, and boarded an armoured train en route to the front. On the journey back, Boer guerrillas attacked the train.

Churchill was sent to clear the line ahead and was able to rescue the engine car, whose driver had been injured. The fighting

BELOW: Churchill (front right) as a prisoner of war just after his capture.

The "Wanted" poster offering a reward for Churchill's capture.

became intense, and he became separated from the troops under fire just down the line. He decided to turn back to hurry up the troops, but soon discovered that he was in an ambush. Scaling up an embankment, for a minute he thought he was safe in the open veldt. Alas he was not – he had run into a group of Boers, their rifles pointed at him, and he had left his Mauser pistol on the train! He was subsequently captured, along with other British soldiers, his friend Haldane included.

Churchill was technically a civilian but he had behaved like an army officer, and he was wearing the holster for his mislaid Mauser pistol when he was captured. The Boers simply did not believe that he was anything other than a spy and he was soon in prison, interned in a temporary prisoner-of-war camp in the town of Pretoria. He was to spend his twenty-fifth birthday behind bars.

Needless to say, he made immediate plans to escape. He and his friends (including Haldane) found an unguarded perimeter spot near a lavatory. Churchill was the first to escape. He waited for his friends but none followed, and then the sentries discovered that something was amiss. A mystery voice from inside the lavatory told Churchill it was now "all up". He interpreted this as meaning it was all right to escape alone, and so he did. He had no knowledge of the language, little money or food, and no compass either. Slowly making his way out of Pretoria, he was lucky to spot a goods train. He smuggled himself on board, jumped off before dawn, and then hid out in the wild, with, as he put it, "a gigantic vulture, who manifested an extravagant interest in my condition…".

After a while, Churchill stumbled across a small house. There was now a major hue and cry for him, with a "Dead or Alive" poster promising a reward for his capture. Thankfully for him, the householder was a British colliery manager who was able to hide his now notorious guest down a mine. Following what must have felt like an age, the manager and some equally brave English coal miners smuggled Churchill onto a wool-transport train. As soon as this crossed the border into Portuguese East Africa (now Mozambique), he emerged a free man and danced with sheer joy, firing his newly gifted pistol into the air.

Churchill was acclaimed as a hero. He arrived in Durban on 23 December 1899 to a rapturous welcome. The war had been going badly for Britain, but here was a brave young man about whom celebration was in order. He became instantly both a famous war correspondent and an officer in the South African Light Horse.

Soon he was a war hero too, taking part in some of the key battles of the Boer War. He helped to liberate Pretoria and won plaudits in the Battle of Diamond Hill. Then in 1900, his life took another turn when the British Prime Minister, Lord Salisbury, called a general election.

ABOVE: A hero's return: after his escape from the Boers in December 1899.

OPPOSITE: Churchill on a pony just after his successful escape from the Boers.

Aylmer Haldane (1862–1950) _____

When Churchill dramatically escaped from his imprisonment by the Boers, he left his companions behind. One of these was Aylmer Haldane, a Gordon Highlander who, like Churchill, had also shown bravery in action in the Northwest Frontier of India.

Haldane felt for much of his life that Churchill had left him and the other British prisoners in the lurch. When *Blackwood's Magazine* libelled Churchill on this issue in 1912, Haldane refused to testify, and his subsequent writing proved he remained embittered. However, this might have been retrospective, since when the team putting together

Churchill's official biography in the 1960s examined Haldane's diaries, they could not find any attitude of hostility on the part of Haldane at the time of the escape.

When Churchill became Colonial Secretary in 1921, in charge of creating what is now Iraq as well as other countries in the Middle Eastern region (see pages 54–59), Haldane – by then General Sir Aylmer Haldane – was, unfortunately for both of them, the General Officer Commanding Mesopotamia. Their mutual past had come back to haunt them...

The Young Winston

Later in his political career, Winston Churchill was often thought of as unreliable. Since two politicians regarded as reliable – Stanley Baldwin and Neville Chamberlain – turned out to be disastrous leaders while Churchill proved to be a success, this is in retrospect no bad thing. The reasons for this attitude towards Churchill may be traced back to the period of 1900–11.

Churchill began his political life as a Conservative MP, for Oldham, in 1900, albeit a trenchant critic of his party's government. After a spell as an Independent, he "crossed the floor" of the House of Commons to become a Liberal in 1904, and found himself working alongside the Welsh firebrand David Lloyd George on the radical side of politics. Churchill and Lloyd George are often regarded as the founders of the Welfare State that still exists in Britain today.

In 1905, he became Parliamentary Under Secretary of State for the Colonies. This was a happy appointment, since his Secretary of State, Lord Elgin, was in the House of Lords, which meant that Churchill represented the department in the House of Commons. While Churchill's views on non-white races always remained Victorian, it is also true that he was concerned for the human rights of those over whom Britain ruled. He resolutely opposed the "disgusting butchery of natives" and wrote that the British should "have only one measure

for treating people subject to our rule, and that a measure of justice".

It was during this period that Churchill developed a quirk which would become one of his hallmarks. While inspecting Uganda, he insisted on giving dictation while in the bath! The Governor of Uganda was, alas, not as amused at this habit as President Franklin Roosevelt was to be more than three decades later…

A few years into his career as an MP, Churchill was invited to stand for Manchester North West, winning the seat in 1906. In 1908, he became President of the Board of Trade, a Cabinet post. In those days this involved seeking re-election at a by-election. Churchill lost his seat in Manchester – his erstwhile Tory colleagues regarded him as a traitor – but he was soon elected as MP for Dundee, a position he held until 1922.

The years 1908–11 (his tenure at the Board of Trade, and then

ABOVE: Churchill (foremost in top hat) ordered police to use guns to remove a group of anarchists from a house in Sidney Street in the East End of London in 1911. He turned up to oversee operations and was regarded by many as going over the top in the use of force.

OPPOSITE LEFT: Churchill was ambivalent about votes for women and the attacks on him and others in power turned him against their cause, to the sorrow of his wife and suffragette friends such as the imprisoned Lady Lytton.

OPPOSITE RIGHT: Churchill in Germany, *c.*1900, watching army manoeuvres with the German Kaiser, later Britain's enemy.

as Home Secretary in 1910–11) are interesting as the time during which Churchill was firmly at the radical end of British politics. This is something often forgotten, since he is now an icon of the conservative right in both Britain and the United States.

He threw himself into welfare reform, in collaboration with David Lloyd George, who had been appointed as a reforming Chancellor of the Exchequer. While national insurance and pension rights were under the Treasury, Churchill was instrumental in helping to introduce them, thereby creating the origins of today's Welfare State. He was keen to help those who "fall from the scaffolding of modern life", to aid the plight of the socially disadvantaged and thereby improve the "stability of the whole".

Churchill is famous for saying that he did not want to be locked up in a soup kitchen with the zealous reformer Beatrice Webb (who founded the Fabian Society with her husband Sidney Webb). Not so well known is the fact that he was a regular visitor to the political salon the Webbs ran together, though since Beatrice was highly abstemious that would have been hard for the bon viveur Churchill had now become.

His conduct at the Home Office has become unfairly notorious. When foreign anarchists in London's Sidney Street began firing at outsiders, Churchill called in not only the police but also the army. He could not resist being photographed at the scene, a piece of showmanship that has become iconic. Similarly, when there were riots in the Welsh mining area of Tonypandy (near Pontypridd), calls were made for more than just the police to deal with it. However, here Churchill is innocent of later calumnies: he was able to prevent the local military authorities from dispatching regular troops to quell the disturbances (though he allowed the cavalry to calm things down). Events became exaggerated in the telling: the political left in Britain was to hold what never actually happened against Churchill for many years.

David Lloyd George (1863–1945)

Although David Lloyd George is now not very well remembered, he has a claim – beside Churchill – to have been one of the two greatest political leaders of the twentieth century. Born in North Wales, at the opposite end of the social spectrum from Churchill, Lloyd George became a lawyer and then MP for Caernarvon from 1890 until 1944. He was originally on the radical side of the Liberal Party, so his appointment as Chancellor of the Exchequer in 1908 was a bold move. His People's Budget of 1909 introduced radical social welfare reforms, thus arousing the wrath of the House of Lords, which vetoed it. This created a constitutional crisis that lasted until 1911, when Lloyd George and Churchill, among others, helped clip the wings of the upper chamber. From 1908, the two men were close political allies.

In 1915, Lloyd George became Minister of Munitions and it was soon evident that he was much better placed to run the war than the lacklustre H H Asquith. In 1916, a political coup put Lloyd George in Downing Street – it can be said that the Liberal Party never really recovered from the split thus created with Asquith. It was Lloyd George who brought Churchill back to office – also as Minister of Munitions – in 1917, and the two remained close colleagues until the collapse of the government in 1922.

Thereafter their paths diverged, but they remained friends. When Lloyd George died in 1945, Churchill paid him fulsome tribute – after all, it was the mechanics of government changes made in 1916 by Lloyd George that enabled Churchill to do so much after 1945.

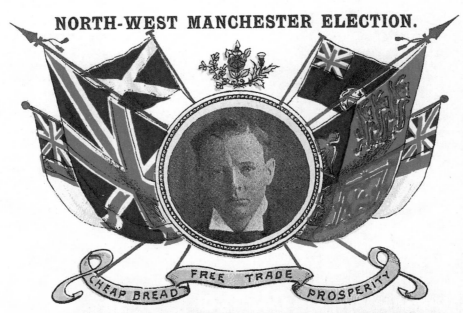

NORTH-WEST MANCHESTER ELECTION.

CHEAP BREAD FREE TRADE **PROSPERITY**

Your VOTE and SUPPORT are requested for

WINSTON S. CHURCHILL, THE LIBERAL AND FREE TRADE CANDIDATE.

Printed and published by W. Hough & Sons, 2, Swan Court, Manchester.

Churchill had left the Conservative Party over the key economic issue of free trade policy, so it is significant here that he describes himself to his voters not just as "Liberal" but also as the "Free Trade candidate".

WAR & PEACE

First Lord of the Admiralty

In 1911, Winston Churchill was appointed First Lord of the Admiralty, a post no longer in existence but which at the time meant that he was the minister in charge of the Royal Navy. Historically Britain had always been a naval power, and when Churchill took office, the navy was at the heart of the Empire and its defence system.

Aside from Churchill's brilliant technical innovations (discussed later in this book), the key achievement of Churchill's tenure at the Admiralty was that he had fully prepared the Royal Navy for war when hostilities began in August 1914. This was no easy feat. Up until the beginning of the twentieth century, it was through its uncontested naval supremacy that Britain really did rule the waves. Then, around 1900, an arms race began between Britain and Germany, the latter a relatively new European power that wanted its place in the sun.

Soon there was a new naval standard battleship, the Royal Navy's *Dreadnought*, commissioned in 1906 as a result of the naval construction reforms introduced by the First Sea Lord, Sir John "Jacky" Fisher. It was far bigger, and with better guns and superior steel technology, than anything that had gone before.

However, the problem was that other countries were also trying to build *Dreadnought*-standard battleships of their own, in particular Germany. Soon people in Britain were agitating for "we want eight and we won't wait!". While the Royal Navy's overall numerical superiority was never challenged, the fact that the German navy might catch up with more modern designs was a major threat, and no one did more to prevent this happening than Churchill. For example, no fewer than nine of the battleships that fought at the Battle of Jutland in 1916 were built for service during Churchill's time at the Admiralty.

Life as First Lord of the Admiralty was pleasant for Churchill

OPPOSITE: Churchill as First Lord of the Admiralty at the launch of the new battleship *Warspite* in 1913.

BELOW: First Lord of the Admiralty Churchill and Admiral Lord Fisher on their way to the launch of HMS *Centurion* in 1911.

John "Jacky" Fisher (1841–1920)

Admiral of the Fleet Sir John Fisher (later 1ˢᵗ Baron Fisher of Kilverstone) was one of the great reformers of the Royal Navy in the early twentieth century. In 1904–10 he served as the First Sea Lord, the head of the naval profession. It was during this time that many major technical innovations were introduced, most notably the new battleship the *Dreadnought* which enabled Britain to keep ahead of Germany in the arms race that marked the years before the First World War.

Fisher had retired by the time Churchill became First Lord of the Admiralty in 1911, but he was very much an *eminence grise*, advising Churchill behind the scenes. Then in 1914, the First Sea Lord, Prince Louis of Battenberg, had to resign in a wave of anti-German sentiment, despite his close links with the royal family (who were also worried about their own German ties). In what seemed a dramatic move at the time, Churchill recalled Fisher as First Sea Lord, although he was well past retirement age. But, as the debacle of the Dardanelles campaign unfolded, Fisher became unhappy and resigned, thereby making things much worse for the increasingly beleaguered Churchill, who now lost his own job. The dream partnership ended as a nightmare for both of them.

1 S.L

"And thus the native hue of resolution
"Is sicklied o'er by the pale cast of
                                    thought,
"And enterprises of great pith & moment
"With this regard their currents turn away
"And lose the name of action"]

=

"We are defeated at sea because
our admirals have learned –
when I know not – that war
can be made without running
risks "
                    [Napoleon].

                    WSC
                    8.4

Churchill loved to encourage his commanders to greater things – and in wartime to
take risks. In this instance he writes to the First Sea Lord Jacky Fisher to urge the
Royal Navy to take war to the enemy, employing even Napoleon in his aid. He was to
do the same with his often-cautious commanders in the Second World War as well.

and Clementine, made all the more so by the birth of their second child, Randolph, in 1911. Admiralty House, at one end of Pall Mall, was one of the smartest places to live in the centre of London. The Royal Navy ship the *Enchantress* was at Churchill's disposal and he took full advantage of its luxurious facilities by going on several cruises, a predilection for which he was teased in the press.

One of his key reforms was to introduce a naval staff – this was comparatively recent in the army but had been unknown in the navy – and he attempted to promote officers on the basis of merit. Needless to say, this did not endear him to the old guard, who disliked the fact that he talked to ordinary ranks when he visited ships and not just to the socially superior officer class.

Technical experts disagree as to how far Churchill had been able to speed up the modernization process by August 1914. But one can say this: while there was no equivalent to the Battle of Trafalgar during the war – Jutland is best described as a draw – the Royal Navy was never defeated. Nor could an economic blockade be imposed upon Britain in the same way that a highly effective blockade was eventually to starve the Germans into submission. And while there were losses, there was no naval equivalent to the Battle of the Somme and the carnage on the Western Front.

One wild episode for which Churchill was criticized was his decision to commit the 1st and 2nd Naval Brigades to the defence of the Belgian city of Antwerp against German capture. In fact, it proved impossible to save the city though it is now argued that the move gained the nearby British Expeditionary Force much-needed time. Churchill went to Antwerp and at one stage even offered to resign his Cabinet post to command the troops himself, a suggestion that his bemused Prime Minister instantly rejected.

On one thing Asquith and Churchill did agree – that the carnage emerging on the Western Front was unacceptable in terms of the human cost. Just after Christmas 1914, Churchill told the Prime Minister that an alternative was urgently required to "sending our armies to chew barbed wire in Flanders". In this Churchill was surely right, and indeed the bloodbath was to become far worse as the war progressed. The problem was to think of a legitimate alternative that would enable Britain and its allies to attack Germany from another spot. This was something in which Churchill believed deeply, and was to do so again during the Second World War when fighting the Germans in North Africa and in Italy. It was a respectable military strategy with antecedents going back centuries, including to Winston's great ancestor John Churchill.

RIGHT: Churchill, in the uniform of First Lord of the Admiralty outside a restaurant in Antwerp where he was sent to assess the situation in the early months of the First World War, October 1914.

He therefore came up with what he thought was a brilliant plan – to attack not Germany directly but its Ottoman Turkish ally, and in particular the potentially vulnerable capital, Constantinople (today's Istanbul), which could be overcome by a naval assault through the Dardanelles. This would also be of enormous strategic aid to Britain's ally Russia, since the two allies could then link up and invade Germany from the rear. Even the great Lord Kitchener, now Secretary of State for War, felt that it could be a war-winning enterprise, so Churchill was far from alone in his enthusiasm.

Historians have analysed the merits of Churchill's brainwave ever since. It probably was an idea too far, but the real problem was that there was no coordination between the Royal Navy and the army (including the ANZAC troops from Australia and New Zealand).

The naval bombardment began in February 1915, but many battleships were sunk by mines, so the fleet withdrew. This turned out to be a mistake, as it left the Turkish defences intact and also alerted the Turks to an Allied attack. When troops were landed near Gallipoli in April, the Ottoman army was ready for them. Instead of a breakthrough, all that actually happened was that the trenches of Flanders were replicated by the new trenches in Gallipoli, and with similar results: carnage and immobility.

Although the Gallipoli idea had been Churchill's, the execution was only partly his responsibility, Lord Kitchener having backed his plan. Churchill was responsible only for the Royal Navy, and cannot

LEFT: ANZAC (Australia and New Zealand Army Corps) troops in a trench at Gallipoli use a periscope to try to locate the enemy.

ABOVE: Allied troops at Gallipoli.

BELOW: Troops en route to fight at Gallipoli.

ABOVE: Rupert Brooke (1887–1915), the renowned First World War poet, photographed in 1914. He died from an infection on his way to take part in the Gallipoli landing.

be held accountable for the chaos of the attack or for the ANZAC casualties. So when the troops had to scuttle back home in January 1916, he should have escaped censure.

However, there were 73,000 British casualties, while ANZAC casualties totalled over 36,000. A vicious political game of pass the parcel ensued, with a search for scapegoats. Lord Fisher resigned in May 1915 and after that Churchill's own job became politically untenable – he was shunted to a minor government post, in effect in disgrace.

As Clementine later told Sir Martin Gilbert, Churchill's official biographer, the "Dardanelles haunted him for the rest of his life… I thought he would die of grief." And since Churchill went out of his way to defend himself, it has become a major object of interest ever since, especially in Australia and New Zealand, where the memory of the ANZAC deaths remains raw to this day.

At the same time an even bigger military disaster took place in the town of Kut, in what is now Iraq, when Ottoman forces besieged the British garrison. This was the worst siege in the entire history of the British army, resulting in an ignominious surrender and thousands of British troops dying in the desert at the merciless hands of the Ottomans. Austen Chamberlain, the politician responsible, also had to resign, but he took it quietly, and was within a few years the leader of the Conservative Party, with Kut forgotten as it is today.

So how much of a disaster was Gallipoli, other than to Churchill's wounded pride? As Richard Holmes has put it, the "result has been that a relatively minor episode in a cataclysmic war has received disproportionate attention", not least because of Churchill himself, who "protested far too much". Gallipoli was a terrible episode, but compared to the Battle of the Somme, for example, proportionately it was nothing like as bad. And, as the debacle at Kut shows, neither were the losses at Gallipoli the worst losses against the Ottoman Empire.

Thankfully, however, Churchill never forgot that as First Lord of the Admiralty he was not responsible for the mess created by the army. In 1940, he was to show he had learned his lessons, and to Britain's great advantage. In that sense, Gallipoli might temporarily have derailed Churchill's meteoric career, but the campaign was not fought in vain.

Learning from History

One of the main lessons Churchill was able to observe from the debacle of Gallipoli was the complete failure to coordinate action between the army (controlled politically by the War Office) and the navy (under the Admiralty). When he became Prime Minister in May 1940, he was determined that such chaos would never again take place. Although the post of Chief of the Defence Staff did not exist until 1959, Churchill made himself the first-ever Minister of Defence in 1940, in order to ensure that proper inter-service collaboration took place. While the separate ministries existed until 1964, Churchill paved the way for a united command of the various armed services in 1940, and ensured that the mistakes of Gallipoli never happened again.

Frontline Soldier

Therapy for sorrow takes many forms, and Churchill now took a dangerous course of action – he became an officer on the front line in Flanders, where the attrition rate for officers was often as high as that for ordinary fighting Tommies. The First World War has been called the graveyard of the aristocracy, and it is certainly true that the social class from which Churchill came took more than its share of death and destruction.

Following the Boer War, Churchill had served in the Queen's Own Oxfordshire Hussars, a Territorial Army yeomanry regiment, and had kept active his commission. However, such units were not always (if ever) sent abroad, so he would have to choose another regiment with which to serve. Characteristically, he was not looking for a cushy staff job well away from danger, but wanted to be where the fighting was taking place. Churchill's lack of fear of death has often been remarked upon, from dodging bullets in the Boer War to wanting to land with the troops on D-Day in 1944, or watching the Blitz rather than sheltering many feet below ground. All of these examples show that he was a genuinely brave man, whose fearlessness was real and not for show.

In Flanders, Churchill spent some time at the chateau of Field Marshal Sir John French (later Lord Ypres), whose time as commander in chief of British forces was shortly to finish. French thought that Churchill deserved at least a full brigade to command, but this proved politically unacceptable at home. Newspapers were already making much of a failed politician going to the front, and Asquith duly vetoed the appointment.

OPPOSITE: Churchill at Armentières with Archibald Sinclair in February 1916, while he was commanding the Royal Scots Fusiliers.

BELOW: Churchill, wearing a French helmet, during his period with the Grenadier Guards in France, 1916.

17. 7. 15

Duchy of Lancaster Office,
Lancaster Place,
Strand, W.C.

Darling –

Cox holds about £1000 worth of securities of mine (chiefly Exchequer bonds) : Jack has in his name about £1000 worth of Pretoria Cement Shares; & Cassel has American stocks of mine wh still exceed in value any loans from him by about £1000 . I believe these will be found sufficient to pay my debts & overdraft. Most of the bills were paid last year. Randolph Payne & Lumley are the only two large ones .

The insurance policies are all kept up & every contingency is insured. You will receive £10,000 and £300 a year in addition until you succeed my mother. The £10,000 can either be used to provide interest ie. almost £450 a year or even to purchase an annuity against my mother's life . wh will yield a much larger income at the expense of the capital.

Churchill wrote this letter in case he was killed in action at the Front in Flanders. It shows he would take care of Clementine financially but more important is his concern that if he died she should not give up on life and "grieve… too much."

Of course it will be much better to keep the £10,000 and live on the interest than to spend it on the chance of my mother living a long time. But you must judge.

I am anxious that you shd get hold of all my papers, especially those wh refer to my Admiralty administration. I have appointed you my sole literary executor. Masterton Smith will help you to secure all that is necessary for a complete record. There is no hurry: but some day I shd like the truth to be known. Randolph will carry on the lamp.

Do not grieve for me too much. I am a spirit confident of my rights. Death is only an incident, & not the most important wh happens to us in this state of being. On the whole, especially since I met you my darling one I have been happy, & you have taught me how noble a woman's heart can be. If there is anywhere else I shall be on the look out for you. Meanwhile look forward, feel free, rejoice in life, cherish the children, guard my memory. God bless you.

Good bye.

W.

So, after a short time with the Grenadier Guards, Churchill was appointed by the new commander in chief, Sir Douglas Haig, to command not a whole brigade but a battalion.

He was allocated a regiment from the Royal Scots Fusiliers, one that had just suffered the horrors of the Battle of Loos, sustaining huge casualties. The regiment marched to Ploegsteert, just over the border from France in Allied-held Belgium – the soldiers walking and Churchill on horseback. Ploegsteert is now famous for Churchill having been there and painted it: no major battles were fought there, and for the soldiers who had seen such terrible attrition on the main part of the Western Front, it must have seemed a blessed relief after the carnage they had witnessed. It became affectionately known by the Tommies as Plug Street, and was not far from the town of Armentières (made famous by the ditty "Mademoiselle from Armentières").

While there were some fatalities and casualties at Plug Street, they were far lower than on the main part of the front – 15 dead and 123 injured. Churchill was injured, but in an accident trying to show men how to get through barbed wire. He was very popular with the ordinary soldiers: parcels from Clementine provided them with luxuries they could not possibly have obtained for themselves. However, Churchill's characteristic ignoring of the chain of command did not go down too well with the officers and NCOs – though one officer he met at the front, Archibald Sinclair, became a good friend. Sinclair later served as leader of the Liberal Party and was Secretary of State for Air during the Second World War.

While sanguine about death, Churchill knew the effect that it would have on Clementine if he were to be killed. The intensely moving and also practical letter he wrote her – to be opened in the event of his demise – is reproduced in this book. They were to write to each other countless times, and the profound devotion that they had for one another shines through in the course of their correspondence.

In May 1916, Churchill saw an opening back into British politics, and was able to resign his commission and resume life as a statesman. However, he had seen what life was like at the front: this was an experience that was soon to be of huge importance when he returned to political power as Minister of Munitions in 1917 under the new Prime Minister, David Lloyd George.

OPPOSITE: As Minister of Munitions, Churchill watches a victory parade at Lille in northern France in October 1918.

Field Marshal Haig (1861–1928)

General Sir Douglas Haig (later Field Marshal Douglas, 1st Earl Haig) replaced Sir John French as commander in chief of the British Expeditionary Force in December 1915.

In his history of the First World War *The World Crisis*, Churchill was not kind to Haig, who commanded the BEF until the war ended in 1918. David Lloyd George in his own war memoirs eviscerated Haig's strategy, which he regarded as responsible for the hideous degree of carnage at the Battle of the Somme (where the British army suffered over 60,000 casualties on the first day).

There is a move to rehabilitate Haig. Whether or not that is right, his reputation made a huge difference to Churchill and his Second World War commanders. Haig was protected from political interference by his wife's links with King George V, and by Conservative friends in the coalition government. The war saw rows between soldiers and politicians, but Lloyd George did not have the leeway to fire military men that Churchill was to have during the Second World War. After 1940, it was clear: Churchill was in charge, his leadership indisputable. And no Second World War general would allow the carnage of Flanders to be repeated.

21 Nov. 1916
"Somewhere in France"

My darling,

Here I am in the line. Except for heavy cannonading the results of wh do not come near us, everything is quiet. A few men are hit now & again by stray bullets skimming over the trenches, or accurate sniping. But we are able to walk about into the trenches without crawling along a sap, & even in the fire trenches of the front line there is great tranquillity. We came in last night on a 48 hours spell, then 48 hours in support, & then into the front line again up to a total of 12 days at the end of wh we are entitled to 6 days rest in Divisional reserve. I am att'd to the 2nd battalion of the Grenadier Guards, wh once the g't d of Marlborough served in & commanded. I get on v well with the officers — though they were rather suspicious at first — & all the generals are most civil & kind. I am not going to be in any hurry to leave this reg't while it is in the line, as its Colonel is one of the v best in the army & his knowledge of trench warfare

[second page]

is complete & surprising. All his comments & instructions to his men are pregnant with military wisdom & the system of the guards discipline & hard work — must be seen at close quarters to be fully admired as at a distance altogether. I look forward to an extremely profitable spell of education.

The conditions of life though hard are not unhealthy, & there is certainly nothing to compare with them — except for cold feet.

Gregg is here, commanding a company & I am going to spend the night in his trench instead of at the battalion Head-quarters. I've relieved Raymond to the 3rd B'n, but I did not have a chance to speak to him. I hear he enjoyed himself greatly, & I sent him a message.

A characteristically ebullient letter from Churchill to his wife, written while he was under enemy fire, albeit not at the heart of the Western Front. Knowing what it was like to be in action was a great advantage to Churchill years later when he became Prime Minister.

I want you to get me the
following things, and send them
with the utmost speed to G.H.Q.

① A warm brown leather waistcoat.

② A pair of trench wading boots. Brown
leather bottoms, & waterproof
canvas tops coming right up
to the thigh

③ A periscope (most important)

④ A sheepskin sleeping bag; that
will either carry kit, or let me sleep

[Bertram will advise you on
all these

In addition

Please send me

5. 2 pairs of khaki trousers (ask
Norman Shipwell [?] put to peach)

6. 1 pair of my brown buttoned
boots —

7. three small face towels

Voilà tout

Your little pattern is a boon &
a jet.

The artillery fire is dying away
now as the light fails; & per
contra there is a certain amount
of maxim & rifle fire beginning.

I am writing from a dugout
a few hundred yards behind
the trench where the Colonel &
adjutant live.

The trenches here have been
damnably neglected by the
troops whom we succeeded of
& the sappers are working hard
to make the defences strong
& safe. The local Bosches
appear to be plunged in
sombre — & I trust ill-paid
inactivity.

I am so glad to be free from
worry & vexation.

With fondest love
always yr devoted
H.

3

POWER & EXILE

Churchill the Artist

His unparalleled public service over six decades aside, what is it that makes Churchill so unique as a person, let alone as a politician? It is perhaps the possession of an unusual amount of what a later statesman was to describe as "hinterland", a whole life quite outside the daily fray, a reputation for outstanding achievement completely unrelated to the pettiness of political debate.

Playing the brave soldier was Churchill's way of entering public life on a platform of genuine heroics, and he combined this with a deep literary talent for describing it in articles and books. But in 1915, his plans for an effortless rise to the top – an ambition beyond his father's achievement – lay, so far as he could see, in ruins around him.

Churchill, however, was not as other, less talented people around him. He sought out ways of coping, always aware of the dangers of inactivity and of the effect that lassitude would likely have on awakening his "black dog". As he was to describe it a few years later in his piece "Painting as a Pastime", first published in *Strand* magazine in 1921:

> *I had long hours of utterly unwonted leisure in which to contemplate the frightful unfolding of the War. At a moment when every fibre of my being was inflamed to action, I was forced to remain a spectator of the tragedy… And then it was that the Muse of Painting came to my rescue – out of charity and out of chivalry, because after all she had nothing to do with me – and said "Are these toys any good to you? They amuse some people."*

In a day long before "art therapy" was at all recognized, Churchill's ability to paint (principally in oils; he disliked watercolour) came to his rescue. It was to be a consolation to him not just in the short-term aftermath of Gallipoli, but for the rest of his long and eventful life.

RIGHT: Churchill painting at Chartwelll – he had learned what it took specialists many years to discover: that art is one of the best forms of therapy for lifting the spirit.

The description of how he first began to learn to paint is vintage Churchill. He had artistic friends – the famous painters Walter Sickert and William Nicholson were based near his later house at Chartwell in Kent – but the initial step was provided by the wife of the distinguished portraitist Sir John Lavery. As Churchill describes it:

"Painting! [Lady Lavery told him.] But what are you hesitating about? Let me have a brush – the big one." Splash in the turpentine, wallop in the blue and the white, frantic flourish on the palette – clean no longer – and then several large, fierce strokes and slashes of blue on an absolutely cowering canvas. Anyone could see that it could not hit back. No evil avenged the jaunty violence. The canvas grinned in helplessness before me. The spell was broken. The sickly inhibitions rolled away. I seized the largest brush and fell upon my victim with beserk fury. I have never felt any awe of a canvas since…

Churchill was to take his easels and brush with him everywhere on his travels for the rest of his life, even to "Plugstreet" where he fought on the Western Front during the First World War. From the 1920s onwards, Chartwell and its surroundings were often to appear in his art – he later had a studio in the garden – along with the South of France, a favourite holiday destination. When he was remapping the Middle East at the Cairo conference in 1921, he painted beside the pyramids, while during the Second World War he found time to paint landscapes in North Africa after meeting with President Roosevelt.

His merit as a painter did not go unrecognized. In 1948, the Royal Academy of Arts elected him the first-ever Honorary Academician Extraordinary, a unique award to an artist like no other.

ABOVE: *Riviera Scene*, painted in France in the 1930s, oil on canvas by Winston Churchill. He only ever painted in oils.

OPPOSITE: *Gate in Marrakech. A Man on a Donkey*, c.1950. Wherever he went, he painted to unwind, and this city was one of his favourites.

Churchill the Innovator

Winston Churchill never took a university degree, but it is probable that no other Prime Minister did more for innovation and technology than he did over a 40-year period. His achievements range from backing use of oil instead of coal for Britain's great battleships when he was First Lord of the Admiralty before the First World War to exploiting Britain's development of nuclear weapons during his tenure as Prime Minister in the 1950s.

It is well known that Churchill backed innovative scientists and inventors – affectionately known as his "boffins" – and their development of all kinds of offbeat devices with which to outwit the enemy after 1940. However, his encouragement of innovation actually went much further back than this. Oil enabled ships to go faster and more efficiently, and while the great Battle of Jutland in 1916 was a draw between Britain and Germany, the use of oil instead of coal did the Royal Navy no harm. (The need for oil also changed the geopolitics of the Middle East – Churchill was among those who laid the foundations for the transformation of Anglo-Persian Oil into the giant company we now call BP when he persuaded the government to buy controlling shares in the company.)

Churchill's time as Minister of Munitions in 1917–19 was also pivotal to Britain winning the First World War; as he would in

1940–45, he visited the key battlefields as often as possible to see for himself what could be done. While it is probably the case that it was the entry of the United States into the conflict in 1917 that ultimately tipped the scales in the Allies' favour, it is also true to say that the invention of the tank – something urged and encouraged by Churchill as the responsible minister – was of considerable help

OPPOSITE: Churchill as aviator in 1914: he had just flown from Wiltshire to Portsmouth in the plane shown.

BELOW: Churchill was instrumental in the origins of what is now the RAF. Here, a Royal Flying Corps (the precursor to the RAF) plane drops a torpedo, 1915.

in ending the carnage in Flanders. During 1919–21, Churchill was Secretary of State for War and Secretary of State for Air. Unlike the great majority of his political colleagues, he had flown many times – then a risky enterprise – and he was instrumental in establishing the Royal Air Force as a wholly modern and quite separate part of the armed services. Since air power was to make a critical difference in the fighting of the Second World War, its origin under Churchill was one of the greatest innovations in military history, taking Britain from the age of horses and cavalry into the vanguard of modern warfare. As his friend Lord Beaverbrook wrote of him during this time, he was always "bold and imaginative in the sweep of his conceptions, prolific of new ideas, like a machine of bullets…".

However, it was as Prime Minister, during 1940–45, that Churchill's love of technology and its possible uses came into its own. Even if he were not directly involved with innovations – as was the case with the bouncing bomb designed for the Dambusters raid by the aviation engineer Barnes Wallis – Churchill created the kind of environment where ideas that would hitherto have been dismissed as preposterous could now find favour, often with tangible results.

Churchill's scientific adviser was Professor Frederick Lindemann, the Professor of Experimental Philosophy (or Physics) at Oxford University. He was Churchill's representative in the world of invention and technology, and applied his expertise to controversial issues such as the area-bombing of targets that might include civilians. But while Lindemann was not always right – he was very sceptical about the existence or possibility of V2 weapons, for instance – he was a leading scientist and people could and did approach him with creative ideas throughout the war. Sometimes these inventions were called "funnies" or "Churchill's toys", yet they often worked – as was the case with the explosives that could be adhered to tanks, an idea that the generals had scorned but which Churchill successfully supported in development at the critical phase.

Atomic weapons are controversial to this day, but Churchill was instrumental in backing British research – the MAUD (Military Application of Uranium Detonation) Committee of experts understood this issue even ahead of the Americans. It was Churchill's decision to share every British scientific discovery with the United States that led to the Manhattan Project – the American-led programme that produced the first atomic bomb – being able to get off the ground so quickly.

R V Jones, the scientist whom Churchill backed in his attempt to counter the *knickebein* or German Luftwaffe targeting beams, said of the Prime Minister that when one met him one "had the feeling of being recharged by contact with a source of living power". Churchill's support of technological innovation saved lives and probably helped to shorten not just one war but two.

ABOVE: Churchill on top of a tank in France, after D-Day in 1944. He was instrumental in the development of the tank during the First World War.

Mulberry Harbours

The Mulberry Harbours, two artificial harbours created at Omaha Beach and at Arromanches just after D-Day, have been called one of the greatest engineering feats in history, and certainly of the Second World War. French seaports were heavily defended, and Allied troops needed to have artificial equivalents if the success of D-Day was to be maintained. Although Mulberry A, the harbour at Omaha, was in use for a mere 10 days before it was destroyed by a major storm, some two and a half million troops and half a million tanks were successfully landed as a result of the two harbours, along with around four million tons of vitally needed supplies.

The Mulberries were largely inspired by an earlier idea of Churchill's, and were developed at his express wish, despite much scepticism. He told the planners: "Bring me the best solutions, do not waste time with the problems, they will take care of themselves..." They took his advice, and the harbours made a vital difference to the war in Normandy.

Winston's Folly:
The Creation of the Middle East

Look at a map of the Middle East today and you will see many of the borders are simply straight lines. Some of this is because the demarcations are between one empty piece of desert and another – a book about the post-1918 colonial occupation of the region is rightly called Empires of the Sand. *But just as the "scramble for Africa" in the 1880s saw a partition of the continent by European powers, one that ignored the people living there, so too was the vanquished Ottoman Empire carved up by the victorious West, particularly Britain and France.*

Much was decided before Churchill was made Colonial Secretary in 1921, but the final implementation of the plans was his doing. Churchill also decided how exactly the rearrangement of the former Ottoman provinces would be drawn, and who the new rulers of the artificial kingdoms would be.

In other words, the map of the Middle East we see today was as much created by Winston Churchill as it was by the infamous "Sykes-Picot Agreement" in 1916 and the Balfour Declaration of 1917 that so bedevil Israeli–Palestinian–Western and Iraqi–Kuwaiti relations down to our own twenty-first century. We live with the decisions of Churchill and a group of British officials (nicknamed by him his "forty thieves"), made in a Cairo hotel in 1921.

One point can be made. Whatever one thinks of present-day rights and wrongs, especially over Palestine, it is significant that in an age in which anti-Semitism was almost normal, in polite English society as well as among extremist agitators in Germany, Churchill was free of all such prejudice, a philo-Semite who profoundly appreciated the contribution of Jewish people to civilization. In the era that would produce the Holocaust, Churchill was a rare beacon of enlightenment.

How did we get to the position in which a British Colonial Secretary in 1921 came to determine the fate of millions of Arabs? In 1914, the British understood that war with the Ottoman Empire would create a major problem for the Raj in India, since millions of its subjects were Muslim and the Ottoman sultan was also the Islamic caliph. So they came up with the idea of finding a genuine descendant of the Prophet Muhammad with whom they could negotiate. That figure was Hussein bin Ali, the Sharif of Mecca.

Sir Henry McMahon, the High Commissioner in Egypt, negotiated with Hussein (the Hussein–McMahon correspondence) and promised him a large Arab kingdom. Hussein then rebelled against the Ottomans, an uprising known as the "Arab Revolt" in which his son Faisal collaborated closely with a British intelligence officer,

ABOVE: Sharif Hussein bin Ali of Mecca, Britain's ally against the Ottoman Turks in the First World War.

OPPOSITE: Prince Faisal, leader of the "Arab Revolt" in the First World War, with T E Lawrence and other Arab leaders in 1919 at the Versailles peace conference.

T E Lawrence

T E Lawrence (1888–1935) was the kind of maverick, individualist genius that Churchill liked, and whom his official advisers cordially disliked. The illegitimate son of an Irish baronet and a Scottish governess, Lawrence's academic brilliance shone at Oxford, and by 1910 he was in the Middle East, spending time working under the famous archaeologist Sir Leonard Woolley.

His fluent Arabic and intimate knowledge of the Middle East made him an ideal adviser for Military Intelligence and for the Arab Bureau established in Cairo in 1914. The Bureau sought an alternative loyalty for Muslims, and in this strategy Lawrence was to play a key role, alongside Prince Faisal. Much of what they did was tiny in military terms, but their capture of Aqaba in 1917 was a huge propaganda success.

Lawrence was a showman, and it is said that much of his book *The Seven Pillars of Wisdom* bears little relation to his war reports. He was also aggrandized in a film by American Lowell Sheppard, *With Allenby in Palestine and with Lawrence in Arabia*. But ultimately he was unable to cope with fame, living under a false name until his death in a car wreck. Whether Lawrence's career was more show-business or actuality, his successes were considerable, and Churchill's support of him says much about Churchill himself.

Gertrude Bell (1868–1926)

Gertrude Bell was educated at Lady Margaret Hall, Oxford, and soon found her vocation as an explorer in the Arab world, becoming famous for her book of travels, *The Desert and the Sown*, about Greater Syria (including what is now Israel and Lebanon as well as Syria), which was published in 1907. When war broke out she was an ideal person for the Arab Bureau in Cairo, where she worked with, among others, T E Lawrence. She then became a protégé of Sir Percy Sykes, one of the leading British officials in the region, being appointed as his oriental secretary, and was based in Baghdad after 1917.

It was from this position that she became one of Churchill's key advisers when the latter was made Colonial Secretary. She was directly instrumental in the kidnapping and removal to exile of one of the local contenders for the throne of Iraq, and the advice that both she and Lawrence gave Churchill in 1921 to opt for a "Hashemite solution" proved decisive.

She continued in Iraq for most of the rest of her life, with a passion for archaeology, and as a key adviser to the new king. She died of an overdose in 1926, and is buried in Baghdad.

T E Lawrence (soon to be nicknamed "Lawrence of Arabia"). But in 1917, the British Foreign Secretary Arthur Balfour also promised a large portion of the same region to the Jewish people for settlement – the Balfour Declaration of 1917 – which directly contradicted what had been promised to the Arabs.

Just to add to all of this, in 1916 Briton Sir Mark Sykes and Frenchman Georges Picot drew up a plan to partition the Ottoman Empire between four of the Allies: Britain, France, Russia and Italy. In fact this plan would soon prove superfluous – the Tsarist Russian Empire imploded with the two revolutions of 1917, and the Bolsheviks denounced all secret pacts, this one included. Not only that, but under this plan Jerusalem would have been under an international mandate and the oil-rich Ottoman province of Mosul would have gone to the French. This was unacceptable to Lloyd George and his government (including Churchill), and it was British and Australian troops who liberated both Jerusalem and Baghdad in 1917 from Ottoman rule. (One of the biggest historical myths of

---

OPPOSITE: A map of the Middle East illustrating the notorious Sykes-Picot Agreement of 1916, a secret agreement between the British and French, with Russian assent, for the dismemberment of the Ottoman Empire. Churchill altered it in 1921 when he recast the region.

---

recent years is that most Arabs supported Faisal, Lawrence and the "Arab Revolt": in fact, as good Muslims they stayed loyal to their caliph, the Ottoman sultan, as Churchill was presciently aware.)

Australian troops also effectively captured Damascus, though Faisal and Lawrence were allowed to think they had done so themselves. But while the British were happy for Faisal to be King of Syria, the French were not, demanding what is now Syria and Lebanon for France. Faisal was expelled, a king with no throne.

So, in 1921, when Churchill became Colonial Secretary and in charge of what to do with the Middle East, he was faced with many choices. He always favoured mavericks, to the despair of his officials, and he insisted on making Lawrence one of his key advisers. He also had delicate negotiations with the French – Britain had now reclaimed the Kurdish-inhabited Mosul from France, and Jerusalem became part of Palestine, the Jewish/Arab area given as a "mandate" to Britain by the newly created League of Nations: a colony in all but name.

On Palestine, Churchill and the (Jewish) British High Commissioner in Jerusalem, Sir Herbert Samuel, stuck firmly to the Balfour Declaration: Jewish settlement was to be allowed, but within prescribed geographical limits since they understood that this was not popular with the existing Arab population.

Jordan – then called Transjordan – was effectively created by mistake. Sheikh Abdullah, Hussein's younger son (thus Faisal's brother), had foolishly collected some tribal warriors together in an attempt to seize Syria back from France.

He was stopped in his tracks near what is now the Jordanian capital Amman and given the "Transjordan" area, former Ottoman territory inhabited by Arabs and not allocated to Jewish settlement. Look at a map of Jordan today – all straight lines and a country with almost no natural resources.

What to do with Faisal was more of a problem, as was the decision on how to deal with three former Ottoman provinces (or *vilayets*): Mosul, Baghdad and Basra. Here Churchill had several options; we forget that countries and borders that we now think of as set in stone were in fact parts of a single huge empire until 1918.

Britain in 1921 was virtually bankrupt as a result of war, and few people were more aware of this reality than Churchill. The British simply could not suppress dissent in Ireland and India – Churchill was deeply involved in the Irish peace talks and 1922 settlement – and keep vast armies in the Middle East as well. Churchill's solution has been called the "Sherifian option", but in fact he was operating in a tradition of the British Raj in India going back to Robert Clive in the eighteenth century: finding loyal local collaborators to rule under indirect British control, like the maharajahs. Not only that, but being the political creator of the RAF, Churchill also understood that it needed just a few planes rather than a British army to keep the region calm and controlled from London.

In deciding how the new region would be ruled, Churchill took T E Lawrence's and leading British official Gertrude Bell's advice, and placed Faisal on the throne, despite the fact that Faisal was not from his new kingdom and that he was a Sunni Muslim, whereas most of the inhabitants of the new state were Shia Muslims. Churchill then merged the three old Ottoman provinces together to create a brand-new country, Iraq. Mosul was mainly Kurdish, and Churchill sympathized with Kurdish desires for independence. However, his Ottoman nemesis at Gallipoli, Kemal Pasha – now Kemal Atatürk, leader of what would become modern Turkey – had reconquered the northern part of what could have been a Kurd state. Thus the Mosul Kurds were joined to the Sunni and Shia Muslims to the south, with the results that we see today.

Britain did save money, as Churchill had hoped. Short-term, the new arrangement – having a client king, like a maharajah in India, and using the RAF rather than the army – worked well. But then, in 1958, the descendants of Faisal were massacred and Iraq fell into new hands.

Back in 1921, Churchill could not possibly have predicted a Saddam Hussein or the Palestinian Intifada. However, the deeds that we do can have far-reaching implications and the way in which Churchill created new states has had profound consequences, still with us today.

LEFT: Churchill's experts in Cairo in 1921: the Mesopotamia Commission (including Churchill, Lawrence and Bell).

Cabinet Minister

The Conservatives' victory in the general election of November 1922 ended the career of the last Liberal Prime Minister, David Lloyd George, and Winston Churchill too found himself among the defeated. During the campaign he had been obliged to spend much time in hospital while Clementine did her best to persuade the voters of Dundee to keep him as their MP. Her efforts were in vain as he, like so many other Liberals, lost his seat. The end of the Coalition also ended Churchill's ministerial career. As he laconically put it that autumn: "In the twinkling of an eye, I found myself without an office, without a seat, without a party and without an appendix."

Without a party... Churchill's defeat caused him to ponder the changing landscape of British politics. One of the results of the split in the Liberal Party in 1916–18, when some followed the pre-war leader Herbert Asquith and others, like Churchill, the dynamic Lloyd George, was that when the Coalition disintegrated in the Conservative backbench rebellion of 1922 – in opposition to Lloyd George's disastrous pro-Greek policy in the war between Greece and Turkey – the resultant election did not just give a large majority to the Conservatives but also relegated the Liberals of any description to third place (a place they have occupied ever since). Perhaps the major change of 1922 was not so much the Conservative victory but the fact that for the first time the Labour Party was the major opposition.

This was unacceptable to Churchill, who was swiftly disillusioned with the now reunited Liberals. After a period of political reflection, in February 1924 he stood without success under his own label as the "Constitutionalist" candidate for the by-election for the Abbey division of Westminster. That year also saw the first-ever Labour government, and also the reunification of the Conservatives, who had split in 1922 over whether or not to continue the peacetime coalition with the Lloyd George Liberals.

In October 1924, Churchill stood again as a "Constitutionalist" candidate, this time for Epping. He was elected and this was to be the constituency that he held for the rest of his political career, until his retirement in 1964. Effectively he had become a Conservative, and after that party's decisive win he was offered, to everyone's astonishment, the key post of Chancellor of the Exchequer by the Prime Minister, Stanley Baldwin. Churchill had coveted this post as a Liberal in 1921, now he held it as a Conservative in a government led by one of the key politicians who had destroyed the Lloyd George coalition in 1922.

Churchill was now back in the party he had left in 1904, and in

ABOVE: Churchill campaigning in Woodford – part of the Epping constituency – in the October 1924 general election, after which he became a Conservative.

OPPOSITE TOP: Winston Churchill and Clementine during the Abbey by-election in Westminster in February 1924: he stood as a Constitutionalist, no longer as a Liberal.

OPPOSITE BOTTOM: Police protect the Churchill-edited pro-government newspaper the *British Gazette* during the general strike of 1926.

one of the greatest offices of state. Seldom can there have been a more dramatic turnaround in British politics. He was to be a Conservative for the rest of his life, although he always retained an affection for the Liberals, and his wife remained a Liberal – albeit a quiet one – even after Churchill became Conservative leader in 1940.

His two major achievements as Chancellor proved deeply controversial. In April 1925, Churchill returned Britain to the gold standard, the then equivalent of a fixed currency (Britain had been obliged to leave the gold standard during the war years). During the prosperity of the "roaring twenties", economically this seemed the right thing to do. However, Britain was forced off the gold standard in 1931 when the crisis of the Great Depression hit all advanced economies, and in retrospect it was perhaps an unwise action to have taken.

In 1926, the trade unions organized what has turned out to be the only general strike in British history to date. Churchill enthusiastically supported his ministerial colleagues in opposing the strike, seeing the issue as a dangerous assault by socialists and not just an economic issue. He even briefly published his own pro-

government newspaper, the *British Gazette*, which, needless to say, he edited himself. The government won, but Stanley Baldwin was careful not to alienate the trade unions, an act of caution that was wise on that particular issue.

The Conservatives lost the general election of 1929, and a second Liberal-supported Labour government came to power. Churchill was in opposition again, but this time as a Conservative. The Labour minority administration supported greater freedom for India, as did many Conservatives. Churchill, however, was not among them, and by 1930 he was not merely out of office but on the back benches as well.

Churchill and the 10-Year Rule

One of the revisionist myths about Churchill is that he implemented the 10-Year Rule which assumed Britain would not be at war for at least 10 years, and could therefore relax about keeping military spending at full throttle. If this is true, then it was Churchill who denuded Britain's defences as Chancellor, only to demand rearmament after 1933.

In fact it is not that simple. Britain, as Churchill well knew as a minister in 1918–22, was effectively bankrupt, and as Secretary of State for War he had already implemented large spending cuts. Britain, with its huge empire as well as home defence costs, simply could not afford, even remotely, that level of spending. The 10-Year Rule therefore preceded Churchill in 1924, and what he did as Chancellor was simply to continue the policies that had been in existence for some time.

In 1925, Britain signed the Locarno Pact with a then democratic (and temporarily prosperous) Germany. Everyone, Churchill included, thought a new era of peace had genuinely come. But German prosperity was based upon the sandcastle of American loans – when Wall Street crashed in 1929, so did the German economy and with it the frail democracy of the Weimar Republic. Hitler's ascent to power in 1933 was not predictable prior to 1929 (the Nazis were then a small, obscure sect), and with Britain itself in recession, increased military spending would always have been difficult. In the context of the 1920s, Churchill did the right thing – what is impressive is that after 1933 he saw that the strategic situation had changed in a way that others, such as Stanley Baldwin, did not realize.

RIGHT: Budget Day: Churchill, Chancellor of the Exchequer, on his way to present the budget in the House of Commons, *c.*1927.

Chartwell

Chartwell, in the Weald of Kent, was the country residence of Winston Churchill and his family from 1924 until his death in 1965. Although the family had different houses in London during this period, Chartwell became a refuge and was the place where Churchill was able to escape from the pressures of life.

Chartwell allowed him to play the gracious host, and was especially useful when meeting those who, after 1933, might not be regarded as giving him wise advice in his opposition to Hitler (the family London homes being too public). It was a bolt-hole, but also the setting for discussion and intrigue, and the physical place that is now forever associated with Churchill in our minds. Churchill had no previous connection with Kent, but it was the part of England from which his devoted nanny had come, and the Weald provided some of the most picturesque landscapes to be found in England. Conveniently too, it was not very far away from London.

Yet, as Churchill's daughter Mary Soames reflects, the house was the one issue over which Winston "acted with less than candour towards" Clementine in their 57 years of marriage, buying it completely contrary to her wishes. As Mary goes on to say, Clementine "determined to make the very best of it" once the decision to buy it had been made, but events soon confirmed her "deep-seated foreboding that they had bitten off more than they could chew". This seemed something to which Churchill was wonderfully oblivious: one year he wrote to his wife, "do not worry about household matters. Let them crash if they will... There will always be food to eat, & sleep will come even if the beds are not made." Needless to say, this did not give much comfort to the financially prudent and responsible Clementine.

The Churchills were not able to move in straight away – indeed this was to take place nearly two years after they first sighted the house, since the entire building had to be renovated. This was something that brought Clementine much despair.

The building suffered from dry rot – the curse of many British homes – and Philip Tilden, the architect that they employed, proved not the easiest of men with whom to work. But all was finally resolved, and Chartwell eventually became the place it is today. For a while, the Churchills also tried farming, and notably had a litter of pigs, but sadly this proved too much to manage alongside Winston's many other responsibilities in London.

In the 1930s, people secretly visited Churchill at Chartwell, passing on to him vital information that they felt he should know. The house was away from the gaze of his pro-appeasement fellow

ABOVE: Churchill contemplating life as he surveys the pond at Chartwell, his place for escape and reflection.

ABOVE: Two famous Britons of the twentieth century – Winston Churchill welcomes a suntanned Charlie Chaplin to Chartwell in 1931. Left to right: Tom Mitford (Clementine's cousin), Freddie Birkenhead, Winston, Clementine, Diana, Randolph and Chaplin.

LEFT: A painting of Chartwell by Winston, giving a good idea of the size and context of the house.

Conservatives. One of his most important informers was Ralph Wigram from the Foreign Office, who was able to deliver much-valued secret information on the extent of Germany's rise under Hitler and the damage being done by the British government's appeasement policy.

Those visiting Chartwell are often surprised by the small size of the library. However, Churchill preferred to work in his study, where he kept all the books he needed for writing his regular newspaper articles and historical biographies. It is perhaps in this room that we can best see the character of the man, since the study is filled with many artefacts associated with Churchill's supreme achievements during the Second World War.

While the drawing room was reserved as a family room, it was in the dining room that the famous discussions – sometimes lasting well into the night – took place. Churchill was always at the centre of whatever subject was being debated and his guests were often selected for their expertise in a particular area.

By 1946, Chartwell had become too expensive for Churchill to run. A group of businessmen led by the press magnate Lord Camrose bought the house and donated it to the National Trust with the proviso that Churchill and Clementine could live there for the rest of their lives. Opened to the public in 1966, Chartwell is now a place that anyone can visit. The spirit of Churchill pervades every room, while the splendid hillside gardens and the lakes he created reflect his love of the landscape.

ABOVE: Churchill and Clementine at Chartwell in 1951 – when it had become a National Trust property – surrounded by their grandchildren, who revere their memory still today.

OPPOSITE: An iconic photograph of Churchill with three of his passions: a cigar in his hand, paint brushes in his pocket and the redesigned part of Chartwell in the background.

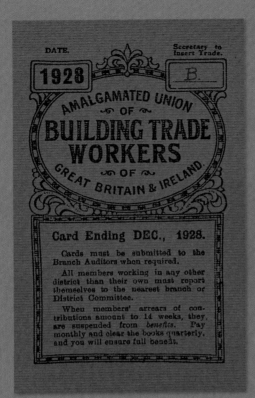

1928

B.

AMALGAMATED UNION
OF
BUILDING TRADE
WORKERS
OF
GREAT BRITAIN & IRELAND.

Card Ending DEC., 1928.

Cards must be submitted to the
Branch Auditors when required.

All members working in any other
district than their own must report
themselves to the nearest branch or
District Committee.

When members' arrears of con-
tributions amount to 14 weeks, they
are suspended from *benefits*. Pay
monthly and clear the books quarterly,
and you will ensure full benefit.

Churchill was an enthusiastic self-taught bricklayer
at Chartwell. But in practice this card was never
used since at the national level the Trade Unionists
strongly disliked his opposition to them two years
earlier during the General Strike. He was given the
card though by the local branch, who were keen to
enlist him.

OPPOSITE BOTTOM RIGHT: Churchill
was rightly proud of his bricklaying ability, as this
photograph shows: many of the garden walls were
built by him unaided.

GENERAL OFFICE .... Branch.

Member's Name ...... WINSTON S.
CHURCHILL

Address ...... Chartwell Manor
Westerham, Kent

Date of Entrance ...... 10TH OCTOBER, 1928.

Section ...... Bricklayer

Payments ⎱ per Week ⎰   Arrears brought frd.
                               from June 30, 19-8 ⎰

Meeting Nights 1928	Officer's Signature.	Levies.	Incidentals Fines, &c.	Contributions. s. d.	Arrears. s. d.
July 7†					
14					
21					
28					
Aug. 4	Bank Holiday	Saturday			
„ 11					
„ 18	*				
„ 25					
Sept. 1					
„ 8					
„ 15					

George Hicks ⎱ Branch
                 ⎰ Secretary.

Meeting Nights 1928	Officer's Signature.	Levies.	Incidentals Fines, &c.	Contributions. s. d.	Arrears. s. d.
Sept. 22					
„ 29‡					
Oct. 6†					
„ 13	James Vague			5 0	
„ 20	Initiation fee				
„ 27					
Nov. 3					
„ 10					
„ 17	*				
„ 24					
Dec. 1					
„ 8					
„ 15					
„ 22	Christmas	Saturday			
„ 29					

† Auditors read Report and Salaries Paid
‡ Quarterly Nights, Election of Officers, &c.

BENEFITS.

The following are the benefits payable in the AMAL-GAMATED UNION OF BUILDING TRADE WORKERS on and after June 30th, 1928.

SICKNESS BENEFIT.—After you have contributed 12 months or more

£1 per week for first 13 weeks.

10s. per week for next 13 weeks.

Then 5s. per week and 2s. 6d. per week according to years of membership.

STRIKE OR LOCK-OUT BENEFIT.—After 4 weeks' membership £1 5s. per week.

Less than 4 weeks' membership 18s. 9d. per week.

SUPERANNUATION BENEFIT.—After you have contributed for this benefit

40 years, 5s. per week.

35 ,, 3s. ,, ,,

FUNERAL BENEFITS.—After you have contributed 12 months or more

If you were under the age of 25 years when commencing to contribute to the fund £20

If you were over 25 years, but under 30 years	...	£17 10s.
,, ,, ,, ,, 30 ,, ,, ,, 35 ,, ,, ...		£15
,, ,, ,, ,, 35 ,, ,, ,, 40 ,, ,, ...		£12 10s.
,, ,, ,, ,, 40 ,, ,, ,, 45 ,, ,, ...		£10
,, ,, ,, ,, 45 ,, ,, ,, 50 ,, ,, ...		£7 10s.
,, ,, ,, ,, 50 ,, ,, ,, 60 ,, ,, ...		£5
,, ,, ,, ,, 60 and admitted previous to June 30th, 1928		£2 10s.

UNEMPLOYMENT BENEFIT.—After 12 months' membership 5s. per week, together with State benefits payable under Section 17 of the Unemployment Insurance Act and the rules of the Society. Juveniles 16 to 18 years of age, half benefits.

LEGAL ASSISTANCE in cases of compensation where members are injured at work, claims for wages, etc.

[P.T.O.

NATIONAL HEALTH INSURANCE.

1. Members should make the A.U.B.T.W. their Approved Society for National Health Insurance purposes, as in the event of Sick Benefit being required it can be paid promptly at same time as Society Benefit. The weekly doctor's certificate will cover both Health Insurance and Society Benefits. Any lad aged 16 can be accepted as members for Health Insurance purposes.

2. Dental and other Non-Cash Benefits can only be granted on WRITTEN application from member. If SANCTION is not obtained the Society cannot be responsible.

3. Members claiming Sickness or Disablement Benefit should send First Certificate and Notice of Sickness to Branch Secretary without delay; the right-hand side of Panel Certificate, "FOR USE BY INSURED PERSON," must be filled up carefully.

4. Approved members can have copies of panel certificates from the Branch Secretary for sending to their Friendly Society at a charge of 1d. This saves paying the doctor at least 1s. for extra certificate each week.

STAR NIGHT.

The "Star" placed beside a date on this card denotes—

1. That subjects of importance or urgency for District, Divisional or National purposes can be dealt with and will have the same status as a special summoned meeting.

2. The nature of the business transacted, number of votes for or against, together with the _total_ number of members present at such meeting, must be sent to General Office.

3. It must be clearly understood that any vote on matters of finance will _not_ be binding unless a special summons has been previously sent to the members.

4. The fine for non-attendance will _not_ be enforceable in respect of "star" meetings.

Private Residence of the Branch Secretary

The Builders, Crescent Grove, South Side, Clapham Common, S.W.4

Treasurer's Name George Hicks

Post Office where Orders should be made payable:

_____

CONTRIBUTIONS.

Section :

1.—Trade only, 9d. per week.

2.—Trade and Funeral, 11d. per week.

3.—Trade and Superannuation, 1/- per week.

4.—Trade, Superannuation and Funeral, 1/2 per week.

5.—Trade and Sick, 1/5 per week.

6.—Trade, Sick and Funeral, 1/5 per week.

7.—Trade, Sick and Superannuation, 1/6 per week.

8.—Trade, Sick, Superannuation and Funeral, 1/8 per week.

1s. per year Political Fund.

General Office of the Society:

"The Builders," Crescent Grove, South Side, Clapham Common, S.W. 4.

Telegraphic Address: "Builders," Clapcom, London.
Telephone: Brixton 4097-8.

Co-operative Printing Society Ltd., Tudor Street, E.C. 4.—6814.

The Wilderness Years

Why was Churchill out of office 1931–39, even though the Conservative Party was in a coalition National Government during that same period? What was at the heart of Churchill's profound dislike of Conservative leader Stanley Baldwin (Prime Minister again 1935–37)?

The Churchill legend has it that he was prevented from holding office because of his resolute and principled opposition to the appeasement of Hitler, and as a result of his clarion call for Britain to rearm in order to be able to take on the Nazi menace. From 1933 – when Hitler acceded to power – onwards, much of that claim is true. But it is not that simple…

From 1931 to 1935, the reason for Churchill's exclusion was entirely domestic. His resignation from the Shadow Cabinet in January 1931 was over the plan to give some self-government to India, and two years before Hitler seized power. India brought out the worst in Churchill, his old-fashioned imperialist side. When referring to the talks between the British Raj and the Indian leader Gandhi, he fulminated against the "nauseating" sight of a "seditious Middle Temple lawyer, now posing as a fakir of a type well-known in the East, striding half-naked up the steps of the Vice-Regal Palace" in Delhi.

As one biographer has put it, during Churchill's resolute and often intemperate opposition to even the mildest form of home rule for India, allied throughout to the most diehard Conservatives, he had "branded himself as an unscrupulous opportunist and a blimpish reactionary".

So when, after 1933, Churchill began to adopt a John the Baptist role of a voice in the wilderness against Hitler and German rearmament – for which we now confer heroic status upon him for his foresight – most politicians and the media ignored him, not because they were singularly short-sighted on the Nazi menace (though that was often the case) but because a mix of Churchill's reactionary attitude to India and a lingering memory of his failures such as Antwerp or Gallipoli had damaged his credibility. He was simply a rogue elephant whose judgment could not be trusted. But he was not without influence – even his disliked rival, the Conservative leader Stanley Baldwin, allowed him to see government material, especially in relation to air strength.

ABOVE: Mahatma Gandhi in Lancashire in 1931. Churchill resolutely opposed even the slightest form of Indian independence.

OPPOSITE: Churchill visiting a polling booth in Epping in the 1931 general election. His "wilderness years" were about to begin.

Churchill and the Abdication Crisis

All his life Winston Churchill was both a romantic and a devoted monarchist. In the crisis in 1936 these two strands merged, and created a major crisis not just for constitutional monarchy in Britain but for Churchill's credibility as a politician as well.

For most of 1936, King Edward VIII's wish to marry his divorced American mistress Wallis Simpson was hidden from the wider public, until a speech by one of the leading bishops leaked the secret and brought the matter into the open.

Churchill foolishly leaped to the defence of the King in proclaiming the monarch's right to marry whomsoever he wanted. But this quixotic gesture was widely misunderstood. Behind the pressure for the King to abdicate lay the machinations of Stanley Baldwin, the Prime Minister, one of Churchill's greatest political foes. Churchill's defence of the King was misinterpreted as a political manoeuvre against Baldwin, a power play, and when Baldwin prevailed Churchill was left isolated.

It also greatly harmed his clarion call for rearmament against Hitler, something upon which Churchill enjoyed crossbench support. People stopped listening to him on Germany because of his support for Edward VIII, and that was tragic.

OPPOSITE: Churchill giving a speech in Paris in 1936, with the aim of reinforcing French resistance to Nazi Germany.

ABOVE: Churchill and the Prince of Wales in 1919. Churchill's support for him as King Edward VIII in 1936 proved to be costly for Churchill's pre-war career.

There is a strong element of tragedy, though, in Churchill's self-exclusion from office, since in opposing Hitler and urging Britain to give up pacifism and rearm properly, events were to prove him triumphantly right. But, as with his other big 1930s blunder – his quixotic support for King Edward VIII in the Abdication Crisis of 1936 – it was largely his own fault, and we should not forget this.

Appeasement – the policy of granting the so-called legitimate demands of the revisionist powers such as Germany – has provoked controversy among historians ever since the 1930s. Now that the Soviet archives have revealed more information, the principled stand that Churchill took against it is once again in favour. He argued against letting Hitler seize the demilitarized Rhineland unchallenged in 1936 and he zealously opposed the callous dismemberment of democratic Czechoslovakia in the Munich Settlement during the autumn of 1938. Germany's invasion of the rump Czech state in March 1939 proved Churchill correct: Chamberlain's appeasement policy was in ruins. And despite his earlier anti-Bolshevism, Churchill's argument in favour of an anti-Nazi pact with Russia is now seen as prescient and might even have been possible had not the viscerally anti-Soviet Chamberlain been in power.

Churchill was right in wanting to drastically increase the size and power of the Royal Air Force – Britain was to win the Battle of Britain in 1940 by the narrowest of hairsbreadths. Sympathetic historians have argued, however, that he should also have asked for the army's size to be increased, since Dunkirk too could have been avoided by this means. But on balance Churchill has been proved right: appeasement did not buy the time that its supporters claimed both then and since, and it is Churchill's case that has been vindicated by history.

Churchill and the Great Republic

For R A Butler, the appeaser and post-war Chancellor of the Exchequer, the ultimate insult to Churchill was that he was a "half-American" adventurer. For Neville Chamberlain, Churchill's predecessor as Prime Minister, one could trust the Americans for "nothing but words". Both these statements, by some of the leading politicians of the time, show the prevailing attitude among the British elite towards the United States right up to the Second World War (and arguably beyond).

Such a view is inconceivable today, even if the United States' power might now be on the decline. But this attitude would also have been unthinkable to Churchill, whom his daughter Mary called a "child of both America and Britain". Churchill's affection for his motherland was not just a wartime necessity. His first lecture tour of the United States was as early as 1900 when he, the Boer War hero, met eminent Americans as diverse as Mark Twain, Theodore Roosevelt and President William McKinley himself.

Churchill lost office in 1929 and he used his new free time to pay the United States his most extensive visit to date: three months with his brother Jack, son Randolph and nephew Johnnie. He visited the West Coast, seeing William Randolph Hearst and Charlie Chaplin. Being an MP, Churchill was able to bring alcohol into the country with him, despite the United States still being firmly under Prohibition. More significantly, he also saw the Bethlehem Steel works in Pennsylvania, enabling him to grasp something few in Britain understood – that the United States was and could be the "arsenal of democracy", an insight that was to prove critical after 1939.

Churchill lost over £3,000 in the Great Crash of 1929. He was in New York at the time, and witnessed the tragic aftermath of the suicide

RIGHT: Winston (right) and his son Randolph (second from left) on a visit to Hollywood in 1930, seen here with British-born film star Charlie Chaplin (in white).

of one of the Wall Street bankers. His own banker Bernard Baruch was still very much alive, and at a dinner the latter organized for the honoured British guest, Churchill was much amused when Baruch addressed him and some distressed financiers as "friends and former millionaires".

Churchill now had to turn increasingly to journalism and writing to make ends meet. His trip to the United States in late 1931, to see Baruch, was to earn him £10,000 from the *Daily Mail* for his articles. On 13 December 1931, he was crossing Fifth Avenue when a taxi hit and nearly killed him. Worse still, he developed pleurisy, and it was not until he was able to recuperate in the Bahamas that he recovered fully. By January 1932 he was back in New York to deliver his lectures, travelling also to Chicago, where even the British press called the trip "a triumphal progress". Everyone wanted to meet him, including President Herbert Hoover, Roosevelt's predecessor.

The idea for *A History of the English Speaking Peoples*, a four-volume history that would become a critical reflection of Churchill's thought on Anglo-American friendship, was already firmly embedded in his mind. But when he told CBS Radio – this was still pre-Hitler – that "I do not believe that we shall see another great war in our time", he was to prove tragically wrong.

By October 1938, however, Churchill was one of the very few who understood that war was now inevitable. On 16 October, he made a historic broadcast on American radio. As he presciently put it:

We are left in no doubt where American conviction and sympathies lie; but will you wait until British freedom and independence have succumbed, and then take up the cause when it is three-quarters ruined, yourselves alone?

In 1939, the defeat of Nazi Germany, as Churchill fully understood, rested in American hands. The wooing of Churchill's "Great Republic" now began in earnest.

BELOW LEFT: Leaving hospital in New York more than a week after his accident, December 1931.

BELOW: Churchill was made an honorary citizen of the US in 1963, but was too ill to be there in person so his son Randolph (next to President Kennedy) accepted the honour on his behalf.

OPPOSITE: Churchill with Clementine and New York politician Al Smith in 1932, atop the recently built Empire State Building.

Bernard Baruch (1870–1965)

Bernard Baruch was one of the foremost financiers on Wall Street over a career that spanned may presidencies in the USA. A leading dealer as early as the First World War, he was an adviser to Woodrow Wilson during that conflict. In the 1930s, he was one of Roosevelt's "Brain Trust" in support of the New Deal and he advised the National Recovery Administration that helped to put the President's ideals into practice. He lived long enough also to advise President Truman.

But it is for his close friendship over four decades with Winston Churchill that he is perhaps now best known. He acted as Churchill's US financial adviser, and was with him when the infamous Wall Street crash took place, precipitating the Depression. Churchill always spent far more money than he earned – to Clementine's constant despair – and it was Baruch who frequently helped to keep his friend financially afloat. The friendship lasted for the rest of their lifetime. It is also proof, if such were needed, of Churchill's strongly philo-Semitism: he strongly disliked the whiff of anti-Semitism prevalent in much of "polite society" in Britain, and consistently supported Jewish friends and aspirations.

Churchill and Family

Winston Churchill was unquestionably one of the most happily married Prime Ministers in British history. This in itself is remarkable.

At the start of his career, many politicians had mistresses, their existence known to the inner circle and hidden by a complaisant press. It is now inconceivable that a Prime Minister could have a mistress actually at 10 Downing Street, but such was the case with Churchill's colleague David Lloyd George, Prime Minister from 1916 until 1922.

There were also leaders who were happily married, but whose wives kept a low profile – how many people have heard of Lucy Baldwin, for example, despite the fact that her husband Stanley Baldwin was Prime Minister three times between 1923 and 1937? Today everyone knows what the wives of our leaders look like, but the same was not true then. Baldwin was happily married but his wife was happiest behind the scenes.

Winston and Clementine were often seen together in public, and showed an obvious enjoyment in being seen as a couple by the wider world. In other words they were a team, and were as much that in private as they were in public – it is perhaps the consistency of their public and private behaviour that makes theirs a remarkable marriage.

Churchill had never been a man of small talk, and before meeting Clementine Hozier he had enjoyed few romances. But he was determined to marry not for position or for money, unlike many of his class who married American heiresses, but entirely for love. In marrying Clementine he fulfilled his ambition.

Take some of the letters Winston and Clementine exchanged while he was at the front during the First World War. They were missing each other sorely and she knew that when he came back to London he would want to get enmeshed in politics. So she wrote on 25 March 1916: "My Darling these grave public anxieties are very wearing – when next I see you I hope there will be a little time for us both alone..." Richard Holmes has written that Churchill's reply on 28 March 1916 was "the most revealing thing he ever wrote". It certainly tells us much about the foundation of his own happiness, his love for Clementine and his degree of self-knowledge: "Oh my darling, do not write of 'friendship' to me – I love you more each month that passes and feel the need of you and all your beauty. My previous charming Clemmie – I too feel sometimes the longing for rest and peace..."

Churchill wished that they could go to some sun-kissed part of southern Europe together, and simply enjoy each other's company,

The TATLER

Vol. XCVI. No. 1252   London, June 24, 1925   PONTAGE: Inland 2d.; Canada and Newfoundland, 1d.; Foreign, 2d.   Price One Shilling

MR. AND MRS. WINSTON CHURCHILL'S DAUGHTERS
DIANA, SARAH, AND MARY

Mr. and Mrs. Winston Churchill were married in 1908, and she is a daughter of the late Colonel Sir Henry Montague Hozier, K.C.B., who was a kinsman of the late Lord Airlie. The eldest daughter, Diana, was born in 1909, the second in 1914, and the youngest in 1922. Mr. Winston Churchill's brilliant political career hardly needs recapitulation. He has probably held more important offices of State than any other living Cabinet Minister

ABOVE: "Mr and Mrs Winston Churchill's daughters, Diana, Sarah and Mary", photographed in 1925 for the cover of *The Tatler*.

OPPOSITE: Churchill boar-hunting near Dieppe in northern France with his son Randolph in 1926.

away not just from the war but also from the hubbub of parliamentary life: "We know each other so well now and could play better than we ever could… I am so devoured by egotism that I would like to have another soul in another world and meet you in another setting, and pay you all the love and honour of the great romances."

Winston and Clementine were to have five children altogether. The first, Diana (1909–63), predeceased her father, tragically committing suicide. Many of her Sandys descendants, however, have become eminent in their own right and have enjoyed the happiness that sadly eluded her.

Randolph Churchill (1911–68) only just managed to survive his father. He is perhaps a tragic example of how great men often do not have equally distinguished sons. As the writer Richard Holmes once put it so well, there "is always a price to pay for greatness, and the great seldom pay it all themselves". Randolph and his father were close – Churchill was determined to have a much better relationship

with his children than he had shared with his own father – but they also spent enormous amounts of time quarrelling, before then making up. (Apparently nannies did not last long in the Churchill household because of the noise level created by the exuberant children!)

Winston's son had many gifts – he was a fine writer, for example – but he was never able to escape the paternal shadow. He was tremendously loyal to his father and his reputation, as Churchill himself had been to his father. Randolph was the author of the

ABOVE: Churchill at Randolph's first wedding, in October 1939 – to Pamela Digby, who later married American statesman Averell Harriman.

OPPOSITE: Family group on Clementine's birthday in 1963: Winston and Clementine with daughter Mary Soames and granddaughter Edwina Sandys.

first two volumes of the posthumous official biography, which was continued by the historian Sir Martin Gilbert after his death.

Randolph only served one brief term in Parliament, in 1940–45, before losing his seat in the Labour landslide election. He was a much-valued commentator on the political scene, but never, alas for him, a player in his own right. He had his father's love of strong drink but without the latter's ability to hold it, and his own marital history was, so unlike that of his parents, distinctly chequered. His first wife, Pamela Digby, went on to have affairs with many famous men and ended up married to Roosevelt's wartime emissary Averell Harriman, whose mistress she was during part of the war. The descriptions of Randolph in Evelyn Waugh's diaries during their stay as special agents behind enemy lines in Yugoslavia make for sad reading.

The Churchills' next child, Sarah (1914–82), outlived her parents by some years, but she too was unable to find their secret of marital happiness. Churchill was not at all happy with her marriage to the émigré actor Victor Oliver, which did not survive the war. (It is joked that Churchill sympathized with Mussolini for shooting his son-in-law, but this may be apocryphal…) As an actress and dancer, Sarah followed a different career to that expected of someone from her background, and never achieved the recognition she perhaps deserved. She was very open about her alcohol dependency in her 1981 autobiography *Keep On Dancing*.

Marigold (1918–21), the Churchills' much-loved and deeply cherished fourth child, was nicknamed "Duckadilly". She died tragically young of septicaemia, to the intense grief of both her parents.

Mary was born in 1924, and at time of writing is still alive. She and Churchill are the only non-royal father-and-daughter Knight and Lady of the Order of the Garter. She inherited the stability and balance of her mother, and was frequently at her father's side during the Second World War. She married a young officer, Christopher Soames, who was in many ways like an extra son for his distinguished father-in-law. The couple lived near Chartwell for a while, and then Christopher went into politics, and managed to have the kind of successful career that eluded Randolph – he served in the Cabinet, as British ambassador to France and as a vice-president of the European Commission. The Soameses' son Nicholas is a prominent Conservative politician, their other son Rupert a well-known businessman and their daughter Emma an eminent journalist.

Mary Soames, along with some of her nieces and great-nephews, has helped to keep the Churchill flame alive, and has been involved in many of the organizations established to honour her father's memory. One of her happier tasks was the editing of the private correspondence of her parents.

Clementine Churchill (1885–1977)

More than just a political wife, Clementine Churchill (née Hozier; later Baroness Spencer Churchill) was a strong-minded and independent companion to whom Winston was utterly devoted for the 56 years of their marriage.

While Clementine's mother, Lady Blanche Hozier, was of aristocratic birth and with some court connections, her father Henry Hozier, a Lloyd's insurance underwriter, was decidedly non-aristocratic and middle-class. Clementine therefore brought no social or material advantages to her husband when they married in 1908. But she did bring total devotion, endless patience with his many foibles, a sharp and critical mind – which Churchill valued enormously – and a sense of stability and fiscal prudence, both of which had been completely absent not only from his childhood but also from hers. As the former Churchill archivist Piers Brendon has aptly put it: "Clementine was the rock on which Churchill's life-long domestic happiness was built. His fidelity to her never wavered and her own never really faltered... Whatever the triumphs and disasters of his political career Churchill knew that he could always rely on his wife's devotion, courage and integrity."

During the war, Clementine was a pioneer. Neither H H Asquith's wife Margot (his second) nor David Lloyd George's wife (who stayed mainly in Wales) was involved much in public affairs during the First World War. By contrast, Clementine immersed herself in many causes, including that of aid for the Soviet Union after 1941, and acted in her own right in many areas.

Clementine never minced her words, and when she felt Winston was not listening to her, would write him memoranda. She also remained faithful to her political beliefs – while he slipped back into the Conservative fold after 1922, she remained loyal to her Liberal/radical views for the rest of her life.

OPPOSITE: Churchill having fun with his top hat – with his daughter Mary in wartime London, 1943.

RIGHT: Churchill at the wedding of his daughter Mary to Christopher Soames in 1947 at St Margaret's, Westminster.

Churchill was very indulgent as a parent, perhaps too much so, and especially in relation to his son, whose boorish behaviour often alienated people. Clementine was naturally stricter, and had firm views on her husband's friends – she liked Frederick Lindemann (later Lord Cherwell), for example, but was very suspicious of Brendan Bracken and Lord Beaverbrook, perhaps with good cause. Bracken was a maverick politician but also a distinguished journalist, who enjoyed the entirely false rumour that he was Churchill's illegitimate son. Lord Beaverbrook was a brilliant newspaper proprietor but known for his raffish ways and, while an outstanding Minister of Aircraft Production during the Second World War, he was also someone whom Clementine could never bring herself to trust. On such matters she was no wilting violet and always made her feelings more than clear. But looking after so powerful a personality as Churchill's was rather all-consuming, and the children perhaps suffered as a result.

Before marriage & shortly after

TELEGRAMS—WEST LONDON—OOLNEY.
TELEPHONE 2 P.O. ST. ALBANS.

SALISBURY HALL,
ST ALBANS.

My sweet Amber dog
    I slept quite well
I don't want to go
to London at all
but must go
immediately i.e in
about an hour –
    No I can't come
back to-night my
precious one & you
are to be good & stay

Clementine and Winston Churchill were a love
match for over five decades, and used animal
illustrations to coo lovingly to each other: she is the
kitten, whose blazing eyes are hidden by turning
away from the viewer. This is so typical of countless
happy love letters.

here & be quite
calm—
    Your loving
Puss Cat

This is the cat—not so good as
your dog, but her eyes
are flashing so that she
is obliged to turn her
back.

Clemmie

Queen's Hotel
Dundee

17 Oct 1909

Board of Trade,
Whitehall Gardens.
S W

My darling.

This hotel is a great trial to me. Yesterday morning I had half eaten a kipper when a huge maggot crept out & flashed his teeth at me! Today I could find nothing nourishing for lunch but pancakes. Such are the trials wh great & good men endure in the service of their country!

The meeting yesterday passed off well. I made a dull but solid speech wh was received most respectfully by a large audience who had gathered at this tiny village among the hills from all parts of Perth & Fifeshire. The Suffragettes arrived in a motor-car and were much pelted with mud by angry ploughmen. Within the meeting all was still.

I find everyone here in high spirits & full of fight. I am endeavouring to restrain them from

running a second Liberal candidate to turn out the Labour man. It is too soon to decide now. There are many inquiries after you, & I have tactfully explained that you are recuperating.

You must read Wells's new book "Ann Veronica". Massingham tells me (this is most secret) that Wells has been behaving very badly with a young Girton girl of the new emancipated school – & that serious consequences have followed. The book apparently is suggested by the intrigue – these literary gents!!

The P.M. writes me that the K. got nothing out of the Tory leaders except that they had not yet made up their minds: which was just the answer he might

Churchill hated being away from his wife and he wrote this while staying in a boring hotel in his constituency in Dundee. He was clearly not yet an artist, but his dog is clearly devoted to Clementine!

have expected. (This is even more
secret, though less libellous than
the hells item)

I hope the Burgundy has reached
you safely & that you are
lapping it with judicious
determination.

I slept in the train without any
ferment like a top. Really that
must be considered a good sign
of nerves & health.

I am glad the P.K.3 vaccination
has taken. Poor little wow, I
expect she will have a lot of
discomfort in the next few
days.

My sweet cat - devote yourself to
the accumulation of health.
Dullness is salutary in
certain circumstances. I
wish you were here, but I am
sure you will not afterwards
regret this period of repose.

The post goes early. & I want
to have a walk before it gets
dark. so I write and now with
tender love & many kisses
from your devoted & loving husband
W

The serious pug

LIFE

BRITAIN'S WARLORD

APRIL 29, 1940 **10** CENTS

4

HIS FINEST HOURS

Winston is Back

With the outbreak of war on 3 September 1939, Winston Churchill came back to office as First Lord of the Admiralty, the minister in charge of the Royal Navy. This was the post he had held in 1911–15, from which he had been cast out because of the failures at Gallipoli. Now, after a decade in the political wilderness, he was back in office. It is said that when the announcement was made of his return, the Royal Navy was signalled: "Winston Is Back!" (Some have doubted this is true, but the spirit of the signal certainly reflected a happy perception, even if the story is merely legend.)

The period 1939–40 is rightly called the "Phoney War" since very little happened on the Western Front, certainly in comparison to events after Hitler's invasion of France in May 1940. On the Eastern Front, a great deal took place, and we must remember that during 1939–41 the Soviet Union and the Third Reich were all but allies. Poland was carved in two, hundreds of thousands of Poles were killed by the Soviet Union as well as by the Nazis, and the Baltic states were conquered by the Soviet Union. There were, in fact, extraordinary plans for Britain and France to bomb the Soviet oil fields in Baku – now in Azerbaijan – which Churchill supported but which were thankfully never carried out.

Astonishing as it may seem to us today, there was a feeling then that the war could be won, and in two ways: first, economically, through an Allied blockade against Germany, and second, on the periphery (including, for example, in the Balkans), something upon which Britain's ally France was very keen.

This lackadaisical approach was symptomatic of the wider peacetime-thinking malaise that characterized the lacklustre Chamberlain regime – something that Churchill was triumphantly to overturn after May 1940. Churchill was now also obliged to be a team player, and here he did his best to be loyal to the second-rate politicians he had so vigorously attacked for the past six years. Nevertheless, containing his sheer dynamism and energy was not an easy task, and thankfully for his talents he was made chairman of the Military Coordinating Committee in April 1940.

By February 1940, it had become apparent that neutral countries in Scandinavia were supplying much-needed iron ore to the Third Reich. Churchill was very aware of this and realized that it might be possible to prevent the supplies from getting through by naval action. That month he had already transgressed neutral Norwegian waters with the rescue of British prisoners of war from a German ship, the *Altmark*. Now he planned a much bigger operation that would result in Norway's neutrality being breached altogether, by laying mines that would prevent the ore from reaching Germany by sea.

Unfortunately for the Norwegians, the Germans were ready to invade to prevent British action from becoming effective.

The Nazi invasion began on 8 April and Norway, while doing its best, was soon overwhelmed. Britain tried to counter the attack by landing troops in Narvik. But soon the attempt to match the Germans proved impossible, and Allied forces were obliged to make an ignominious withdrawal from Norway, which now fell wholly into Germany's clutches.

This was, by any account, a complete fiasco, parallel in many ways to Churchill's last tenure of office at the Admiralty and Gallipoli. As his biographer Geoffrey Best puts it, there was no way of concealing that "overall it was a disaster. If the times had been normal, Churchill's responsibility… would have got him into trouble." Such a view is unquestionably correct, but the extraordinary thing is that when the House of Commons debated the Norway debacle on 7 and 8 May, the result was not Churchill's ruin, as back in 1915–16, but his elevation to the posts of Prime Minister and Minister for Defence. It is perhaps one of the most extraordinary turnarounds in British politics.

This was because the war was about to take a turn for the worse. The Phoney War was over: with the invasion of the Netherlands (neutral in the First World War) and then Belgium by Germany, it was clear that real fighting was now about to begin. The key issue, therefore, was not Churchill's mishandling of Norway but whether or not an entirely partisan government led by Chamberlain was any longer fit to run the war. It was therefore the Prime Minister in the dock, not the First Lord of the Admiralty, and gallantly though Churchill defended Chamberlain in the debates in Parliament, everyone knew that if the government lost support, Chamberlain was doomed.

In fact, much of the Conservative Party (and the King and Queen, along with much of what we would now call the establishment)

ABOVE: Churchill as First Lord of the Admiralty in February 1940, welcoming HMS *Exeter* back to Plymouth.

OPPOSITE: Chamberlain's War Cabinet in 1939, with Churchill back in office as First Lord of the Admiralty.

BELOW: The Norwegian town of Narvik burning after Allied bombardment in May 1940 – Norway was Churchill's responsibility.

wanted the Foreign Secretary, Lord Halifax, to replace Chamberlain as Prime Minister, someone who would have been acceptable to the Labour opposition. Thankfully for Britain's survival against Hitler, Halifax realized he was not up to the task. Democracy was safe…

Churchill and Norway

So far as the military side went, Norway was a major defeat for Britain. But the Royal Navy, for which Churchill was directly responsible, inflicted major damage and casualties on the German fleet, such that the latter took months to recover. Therefore, although Norway fell, Britannia still ruled the waves as far as the North Sea was concerned.

When it comes to Britain's survival in 1940, we often refer to the narrow margin of victory of the Battle of Britain as fought in the air. But we forget that, in order to mount a successful invasion of the island in 1940, Hitler also had to have German predominance at sea. This was rendered impossible due to the serious damage inflicted upon Germany's navy in Norway in April and May, with the result that Royal Naval predominance in the North Sea continued regardless of the army's defeats both in Norway and then in France, after the debacle at Dunkirk. (In fact, had the Royal Navy not been all-powerful, the Dunkirk evacuation could never have taken place.)

Seen in his light, perhaps the fiasco in Norway was not such a mess after all.

Finest Hour

The preservation of British freedom in 1940 is the part of Churchill's life for which he is most famous. However, one can argue that he achieved even more than that – he saved Western democracy itself. A Britain that did a deal with Hitler would have effectively granted Hitler an empire from Calais to Vladivostok.

This would have made eventual Allied victory all but impossible. The UK could not have been America's launch pad for the liberation of Europe, so such an event would never have happened. As Churchill said in a lesser-known oration: "I have only to add that nothing which may happen to this battle [as France was falling] can in any way relieve us of the duty to defend the world cause to which we have vowed ourselves…" It was not just the defence of Britain but the "world cause" of freedom and democracy itself.

Not only that, but Churchill saw that it was from the United States that salvation would come. In this he was proved triumphantly right, again something that we take for granted but which was then an idea ignored by the bulk of the British political establishment, for whom Churchill's half-American status was a source of suspicion and not of hope.

Churchill was made to lead in war, a role that would have been impossible for Chamberlain, for whom the end of peace was the destruction of his whole world. As biographers have put it, Churchill

possessed a zest, a sense of energy, of "Action This Day" that the more pacific Chamberlain lacked. Churchill may have been deeply egotistical and impossible to work with, but even these traits were put to good use and provided the dynamism that allowed the British people to believe that survival might indeed now be possible.

It is a myth that Churchill never allowed contemplation of surrender. He himself rejected it utterly, but the government actively discussed it, especially when Lord Halifax's wish for peace feelers through Italy were considered. As Churchill said during those debates, "Hitler's terms would put us completely at his mercy. We should get no worse terms even if we went on fighting, even if we were beaten, than were open to us now." Thankfully, both Chamberlain and the Labour Party supported Churchill and surrender ceased to be an option.

Nowadays we take our eventual Allied victory for granted. But in the grim circumstances of 1940, with the Soviet Union allied in all but name to Nazi Germany and the United States in official isolation, survival looked against all the odds. Here the psychologists are perhaps right: it took someone with a view of British history that at any other time would have been anachronistic if not actually ludicrous to stiffen the sinews and summon the blood of the British people, and enable them to keep going when all looked bleak and hopeless.

Churchill's sheer energy was at the heart of the war effort. He worked literally night and day, dictating memoranda to his secretaries well into the night. He enquired into even the smallest aspects of

ABOVE: Smoking a customary cigar, steel-helmeted Prime Minister Winston Churchill peers through binoculars from an observation post at Dover, to watch the RAF duel with Nazi airmen over "Hell's Corner". He then continued his inspection tour of Dover and Ramsgate. September 1940.

OPPOSITE: British troops being evacuated from Dunkirk in June 1940.

"LET US GO FORWARD TOGETHER"

The Greatest Wartime Speeches
13 May 1940

Churchill is rightly famed for his oratory, a gift that in the television age of instant sound bites is increasingly forgotten. For survivors of the Blitz, of whom there are still many, and their descendants, the words he uttered at the time continue to resonate across the decades:

> *I have nothing to offer but blood, toil, tears and sweat... You ask, what is our policy? I can say: it is to wage war by sea, land and air, with all our might and with all the strength that God can give us; to wage war against a monstrous tyranny, never surpassed in the dark, lamentable catalogue of human crime. That is our policy. You ask, what is our aim? I can answer in one word: it is victory, victory at all costs, victory in spite of all the terror, victory however long and hard the road may be.*

It is important to remember that when Churchill made this speech to the House of Commons, he was Prime Minister but not leader of the Conservative Party, a post still held (until his death later that year) by Neville Chamberlain. Churchill was cheered far more by Labour MPs than by Conservatives, many of the latter still deeply mistrustful of someone they suspiciously regarded as a warmonger and maverick.

LEFT: Churchill at the Supreme War Council in Paris in June 1940, trying to stiffen French sinews: with French premier Reynaud, Sir John Dill and Clement Attlee.

The Greatest Wartime Speeches 4 June 1940 and After _____

The evacuation from Dunkirk was a British defeat, however disguised. But it aroused in Churchill one of his most famous speeches:

We shall fight in France, we shall fight on the sea and oceans, we shall fight with growing confidence and strength in the air, we shall defend our Island, whatever the cost may be, we shall fight on the beaches, we shall fight on the landing grounds, we shall fight in the fields and in the streets, we shall fight in the hills, we shall never surrender.

France fell not long afterwards. Britain was not as alone as legend suggests – there were still the Dominions such as Canada, Australia and New Zealand, and, albeit very reluctantly in the case of millions who wanted independence, the great Indian Raj. But even the insuperable odds of survival did not deter Churchill:

Let us therefore brace ourselves to our duties and so bear ourselves that, if the British Empire and its Commonwealth last for a thousand years, men will still say, "This was their finest hour."

AND THEY WILL SAY—
"THIS WAS OUR FINEST HOUR
THE PRIMINSTER

The gratitude of every home in our Island,
in our Empire, and indeed throughout
the world, except in the abodes of
the guilty,

goes out to the British airmen who,
undaunted by odds,
unwearied in their constant
challenge and of mortal danger,

are turning the tide of world war
by their prowess and by their
devotion.

Never in the field of human conflict
was so much owed by so many to so few.

All hearts go out to the Fighter pilots,
whose brilliant actions we see with
our own eyes day after day,

but we must never forget that all the
time,
night after night,
month after month,

our Bomber Squadrons travel far into
Germany,
find their targets in the darkness
by the highest navigational skill,
aim their attacks,
often under the heaviest fire
often with heavy loss,
at times

with deliberate careful precision,
and inflict shattering blows upon
the whole of the technical and
war-making structure of the
Nazi power.

These stirring words have gone down in history and still have the
power to move those who read or hear them. It is rhetoric of this
power that stirred the British people into defying the odds in 1940
just as the brave RAF pilots were doing in the sky.

government policy, his constant curiosity keeping everyone on their toes.

His 24-hour habits – he catnapped in the afternoons while others continued to work – might have proved exhausting for secretaries and field marshals alike, but the total drive and commitment that he provided were essential to the winning of the war.

His fearlessness was a model for everyone. He would often watch air raids from the roof rather than cower in the bunkers. Indeed he often slept in 10 Downing Street rather than in the War Rooms, spending weekends at Chartwell except during full moon when nearby Ditchley Park proved safer. This too showed ordinary citizens that he was in it with the rest of them.

His relations with his senior admirals and generals have perhaps been unfairly treated because of Sir Alan Brooke's diaries, which often portray conflict and argument. But Churchill's own personal

chief of staff, Sir Hastings "Pug" Ismay, has a far more emollient picture of the intense Prime Minister–military relationship, and Brooke himself, however frustrated, felt that Churchill's contribution was essential to winning the war. However much he argued with the armed services, Churchill always listened to them and never ignored them as Hitler so often did.

ABOVE: Churchill inspecting Grenadier Guards (with whom he had served briefly during the previous war) in July 1940, when invasion was still expected.

OPPOSITE: Churchill and Clementine in the autumn of 1940, inspecting the recently blitzed London Docks. The previous nights had seen some of the heaviest bombing of the capital so far.

The same could be said of his Labour Coalition colleagues –
Attlee made clear in 1945 that without Churchill, Britain could
well have lost. Pre-war ideological differences were set aside for the
overwhelming task of preserving British freedom and defeating the
nation's enemies, a task for which Churchill was ideally suited.

More recently, historians have argued that Britain's position was
not actually as terrible as it seems in retrospect. If so, Churchill's
unstinting support of technical endeavour and expertise could be said
to have been even more important than realized, since it was British
innovation, actively encouraged by him, that beat the odds in the
period from June 1940 to December 1941, after which American
entry made Allied victory inevitable.

We see Churchill's vital contribution in the slender margin by
which the Luftwaffe was defeated in the all-important Battle of

OPPOSITE: A famous photo of Churchill in the ruins
of the House of Commons after it was bombed.

ABOVE: A characteristic image of Churchill with an
American tommy gun in 1940: he told General Ismay
that he intended to die fighting.

Britain in autumn 1940, when he visited an air base and asked where
the reserves were, only to get the chilling reply that *there were none*.
Similarly, during the Blitz, when the morale of the nation could have
been destroyed, Churchill kept hope alive, or as he modestly put it,
gave the British lion its roar.

Churchill's Cigars

Churchill is famous for his iconic cigars. He usually smoked Havanas, for which he had developed a taste as a young war journalist in Cuba, where he had celebrated his twenty-first birthday in 1895. The shop where he later bought them, then Robert Lewis of St James's in London, founded in 1787, is still there under the name of Fox, and still very proud of its most illustrious customer.

By 1940, Churchill was Prime Minister: his cigars, his V for Victory sign and his "siren suits" all became trademarks of Britain's great wartime leader. But now urgent security issues were involved. Were the cigars sent to him from around the world, including admirers in Cuba itself, genuine or poisoned? One senior MI5 specialist, Victor Rothschild of the well-known banking family, was to win a wartime George Medal for uncovering a German bomb hidden in a crate of onions…

Churchill's scientific adviser, Professor Frederick Lindemann, asked Rothschild to probe a particular gift of Cuban cigars in 1941. Bacteriological tests had to be carried out, and correspondence ensued between Rothschild and the Prime Minister's Private Secretary, Jock Colville. All this happened during the course of the Nazi invasion of Russia and Britain's conflict with the Wehrmacht in the Middle East.

No one suspected the Cubans themselves of trying to poison the Prime Minister. But there were known Nazi agents in Cuba. Jock Colville wrote:

> *I have discussed with the Professor, and also with Lord Rothschild of MI5, the question of security and they both insist that however reputable the source from which the cigars come it is impossible to ensure that they are safe. It would be perfectly possible to insert a grain of deadly poison in, say, one cigar in fifty, and although Lord Rothschild can and will arrange for those that arrive to be X-rayed, he would only guarantee them after subjecting each one to careful analysis. This could not be done without destroying the cigars.*

TOP RIGHT: One of the many Churchill cigars to appear at auction. Such are their iconic status that cigars, partly smoked by Churchill, have fetched up to £4500 in the past.

RIGHT: Churchill on one of his many overseas visits during the war, seen here in Middle East/Africa. When viewing his wartime photos, one would think a cigar never left his lips!

Champagne, Alcohol and Dependency

Winston Churchill loved his drink. His favourite champagne was Pol Roger, which he started drinking in 1908 when he entered the Cabinet, but it was not until after the liberation of Paris in 1944 that he began a strong relationship with the eponymous French family that produced the drink, at a dinner at the British Embassy. Every year thereafter, Odette Pol-Roger would send him a crate of his favourite champagne.

Was he, as some have suggested, an alcoholic? Certainly some around him were worried: the austere Sir Alexander Cadogan, head of the Foreign Office, noted at the Yalta conference in 1945 with Stalin and a dying Roosevelt that the Prime Minister was "drinking buckets of Caucasian champagne which would undermine the health of any ordinary man". But was Churchill ordinary? And did his prodigious level of alcohol intake prevent him from making rational decisions, especially in wartime?

Historians are divided, though many agree with Churchill's own assessment that while he did indeed drink a lot, especially when under stress, he had taken more out of alcohol than it had taken out of him. For most people, his intake would indeed be profoundly unhealthy. There is no doubt too that, as alcoholism is well known by psychologists to mask depression, his excessive habit tied in closely with his "black dog" syndrome. He could not do without the support of a stiff drink – often to his more abstemious wife's despair – but we cannot say that he was an alcoholic, or someone whose habits adversely affected the decisions he made about peace and war.

Thankfully for Churchill, a way was found to undertake the tests without all of the cigars being destroyed. After six weeks of testing, MI5's chief expert Dr Gerald Roche Lynch was able to assure Rothschild that the Cuban cigars were safe from "potentially volatile chemical agents" for the Prime Minister to smoke.

Churchill was thrilled. On 19 September 1941, he not only smoked the cigars himself, but also gave one to every member of the Cabinet Defence Committee to do the same. He told them, according to one junior minister present that day:

Gentlemen, I am now going to try an experiment. Maybe it will result in joy. Maybe it will end in grief. I am going to give you each one of these magnificent cigars… It may well be that these each contain some deadly poison… It may well be that within days I shall follow sadly the long line of coffins up the aisle of Westminster Abbey. Reviled by the populace, as the man who has out Borgia-ed Borgia.

RIGHT: Churchill with one of his famous cigars, taken on a trip to the troops in North Africa in 1942.

TOP: Pol Roger's Cuvée Sir Winston Churchill champagne – legendarily his favourite champagne.

The Worst and Best of Times

The year 1941 was to bring much bad news for the Allies. However, it was also the year in which they effectively won the war, for Hitler made the two mistakes of invading the Soviet Union and of declaring war on the United States.

For Britain, 1941 was a military disaster, and this can be attributed in large measure to Churchill's strategic decisions. But having said that, biographer Sir Max Hastings is surely right to say that no British general or admiral could have achieved otherwise at this stage in the war, and Churchill's own responsibility can be seen in that light.

1941 could have turned out very differently. The British general Richard O'Connor's forces routed the Italians in North Africa, and the British and Empire troops there and in Ethiopia came close to eliminating Italy from the continent altogether. Potential early victory against part of the Axis seemed within grasp, but this was snatched away by the decision that Churchill and the War Cabinet in London along with Anthony Eden (the Foreign Secretary) and Sir John Dill (still Chief of the Imperial General Staff) made to support Greece. This was a country already under attack from Italy, and now, as we knew through "Ultra" (the codename for Allied high-level signals intelligence, derived from the breaking of German codes), menaced by Germany as well. Instead of following up on Britain's victories in North Africa, key troops and materiel were sent from there to defend Greece against Hitler's planned assault, a decision fully endorsed by Churchill despite his later denials.

A British-engineered coup in Belgrade briefly held promise that Yugoslavia would support the Allies against Germany. But the blitzkrieg unleashed on that unhappy and divided country, which was conquered in days, ended that hope. The Axis forces then swept through Greece, and the British were forced to leave as quickly as possible, abandoning much of their equipment.

An attempt to hold Crete as an island fortress proved equally futile. Airborne German forces seized the airfields, gaining the advantage, and many British and New Zealand forces were evacuated by a hairsbreadth. Thousands of them were captured and Crete fell.

Simultaneously Hitler, enraged by Italian defeats, sent one of his better generals, Erwin Rommel, and a panzer-equipped army, the Afrika Korps, to turn the situation around. This Rommel did even faster than anticipated, and soon all O'Connor's gains from earlier in the year had vanished, and the now-victorious Axis forces seized the advantage in North Africa.

TOP: Italian prisoners taken in January 1941 during British victories in North Africa.

ABOVE: Wounded British soldiers who managed to escape from Crete in May 1941.

OPPOSITE: A characteristically pugnacious Victory sign to a ship in Iceland, August 1941.

Churchill's attempt to rescue Greece was morally the right thing to do. But Britain was woefully under-equipped and under-manned to fight successfully both in North Africa and in Greece, let alone to guard against invasion at home. The disasters of 1941 – what Sir John Keegan has called a "second Dunkirk" – showed just how perilous Britain's plight had become.

But in 1941 Britain was no longer fighting alone. We now know that Hitler had long planned to invade the Soviet Union, both for ideological reasons and to make use of its oil supplies in the Caucasus and exploit its food supplies. This was a crucial factor, the importance of which historians are only now realizing.

In June 1941 the invasion occurred, codenamed "Barbarossa". Thanks to "Ultra", Churchill knew of the plans, but Stalin, as paranoid as ever, refused to take any notice of British entreaties, with the result that millions of Soviet civilians and soldiers needlessly lost their lives in the carnage of the early invasion.

Churchill had been anti-Bolshevik most of his political life. But now his enemy's enemy was his friend, and casting decades of anti-Communism aside, he made as sure as he could that the maximum amount of supplies reached the beleaguered Soviet Union, often at great cost to the Royal Navy escorts.

Few at the time expected the Soviet Union to survive, and the Wehrmacht failure to capture Moscow was a close-run thing, mainly because at the critical stage Hitler diverted a major part of his forces southwards, towards the Ukrainian bread basket and beyond that to the oil fields of the Caucasus. Thankfully for the war's outcome, Moscow survived, the unprepared German invaders suffered terribly in the freezing Russian winter, and Red Army troops from unconquered territory were able to hold the line.

Modern research now suggests that the Germans could never have successfully invaded a country of the Soviet Union's size and

population – any German army, however good, would have been bogged down sooner or later even if Moscow had fallen. The logistics of conquering the Soviet Union and the limits of the Third Reich economy were simply obstacles far too great ever to allow victory. But Churchill did not know that then. As he put it, "I will unsay no word I have spoken… The past with its crimes… flashes away. Any man or state who fights on against Nazidom will have our aid…"

Meanwhile his wooing of the United States continued apace. In August 1941, he travelled on the *Prince of Wales* (later to be sunk off Malaya) to meet Roosevelt for the first time since their accidental meeting in 1918, this time as British supplicant to America's great power. The two countries signed the Atlantic Charter, an agreement of common democratic ideals and values, but while Lend-Lease aid continued to arrive, and Roosevelt agreed that should America declare war, Germany would be the main enemy, the United States came no nearer to entering the war on Britain's increasingly fragile side.

The importance of Lend-Lease cannot be exaggerated. Britain gained vital military supplies from the USA from March 1941 onwards (and later the USSR was also to benefit). This enabled Roosevelt, who called the support of the UK part of the "battle for all civilization",

to get around the Neutrality Acts passed by Congress in the 1930s and also undermine those Senators who still supported isolationism. (Britain had been given valuable naval destroyers back in 1940 in return for the US gaining Royal Navy bases in the Caribbean – Lend-Lease now made such things official and permanent so long as the war lasted.)

While many of the terms were advantageous to the USA, which gained extra bases, the supplies gained by the British enabled the United Kingdom and its Dominion allies to survive in a way that would otherwise have been impossible. Churchill's achievement in ensuring this was vital to Britain's ability to stay fighting during June 1940 to December 1941, when survival itself often hung by a thread. Every tank and battleship that came through Lend-Lease was a key contribution to keeping the war going, just as Churchill had realized.

Then on 7 December 1941, everything changed. The Japanese attacked the American naval base at Pearl Harbor, thereby drawing the reluctant United States into the war after all. Hitler then made his second-biggest mistake (after that of invading the Soviet Union):

he declared war on the United States. To Churchill's immense relief, this meant that the United States could stick to its Germany-first priority. Roosevelt was able to keep his promise despite many Americans wanting to concentrate on revenge against Japan.

As Churchill put it at the news of American entry, "So we had won after all!... We had won the war. England would live... United we could subdue everybody else in the world. [That night] I went to bed and slept the sleep of the saved and thankful." Victory, as he fully understood, would take time. But as Churchill and precious few others understood, the United States had the unique strength to take on both Germany and Japan. Perhaps this insight into American power was, with his decision to keep fighting in 1940, Churchill's greatest contribution to victory – the next three years, though costly, were to prove him correct.

Within days Churchill was in Washington DC to begin work on what he would aptly call the Grand Alliance, the Anglo-American relationship that would help to win the war.

Franklin Delano Roosevelt (1882–1945)

Franklin Delano Roosevelt (known as "FDR") was the longest holder of the presidency of the United States: 1933–45, winning a unique four terms.

The mood in the USA after 1918 was overwhelmingly one of isolationism, of no longer caring about the quarrels of the Old World. Thankfully for Churchill, Roosevelt did not share this view, and did all he could short of war before 1941 to help Britain and thus the cause of liberty itself against Nazism. In 1939 he declared the USA to be the "arsenal of democracy" and in March 1941 he began Lend-Lease to provide Britain with urgently needed munitions, thereby circumventing Congressional legislation on observing neutrality.

Churchill and Roosevelt had first met in 1918 when the latter was Assistant Secretary of the Navy during the Great War. When, in September 1939, Churchill became First Lord of the Admiralty,

he began an active correspondence with Roosevelt that was to last continuously until Roosevelt's death in office just before VE Day in 1945. It was perhaps the most important correspondence of Churchill's life and maybe of the twentieth century, since it convinced Roosevelt that everything possible needed be done to help the British in their struggle against Nazism. It is worth saying that much of the exchange was personal as well as political: the two men were aristocratic mavericks, regarded as unsound by their social background, but both possessed the profoundest understanding of what they knew to be the most crucial issues of the day. What began formally ended up in true friendship, although Roosevelt's wish to win Stalin over to the cause of the UN later in the war was ultimately to cause much heartache on Churchill's side of the relationship.

PRIME MINISTER'S

PERSONAL TELEGRAM

SERIAL No. *T. 1757/2*

10, Downing Street,
Whitehall.

<u>PRIME MINISTER TO PRESIDENT.</u>

No 241

    Last year I passed a happy Christmas
in your home and now I send my heartfelt
wishes to you and all around you on this
brighter day than we have yet seen.   My wife
joins with me in this message to you and
Mrs. Roosevelt.

                Winston and Clementine Churchill

25.12.42.

Churchill regarded his personal as well as his political relationship
with Roosevelt as being at the heart of Britain's war and this
small note encapsulates the very warm and personal nature of the
Special Relationship.

Nadir and Restoration

The year of 1942 saw the nadir of Britain's war, but also the turning of the tide that would take Churchill and the Allies all the way to victory in Berlin in 1945.

In February 1942, Britain suffered a defeat far worse even than the loss of the Dardanelles in 1916: the capture of the fortress/naval base of Singapore by a Japanese invasion army – much smaller than the British force defending the area – which had cut through British-ruled Malaya far more effectively than anyone could have imagined.

The historian and biographer of Churchill Sir Max Hastings is often controversial when he decries British fighting prowess during the war. But so pusillanimous and weak were the British-Australian forces, and so inept their leaders, that in this case he is surely right. Churchill held the same view, all his pleas for martial valour and heroism falling on stony ground as Lieutenant-General Arthur Percival ignominiously surrendered to the Japanese. As a result, thousands of men became prisoners of war and were to endure the most barbaric treatment. By any account the fall of Singapore was a catastrophe, and one from which British rule in Asia never recovered.

Then, in June 1942, Tobruk fell to Rommel's panzer divisions, a humiliation made worse by the fact that Churchill was visiting Roosevelt in Washington DC when the news came through. Britain's catalogue of military disasters, from Dunkirk to Crete to Singapore, looked unending.

OPPOSITE: The British surrender party being escorted to Japanese headquarters in Singapore in February 1942: one of the worst defeats in British military history and a great blow to Churchill.

LEFT: The "Desert Fox": Field Marshal Erwin Rommel, in North Africa in 1942.

BELOW: Churchill wooes the crowds in Washington DC in 1942 before his address to Congress.

April 3
11 pm

Dear Winston

What Harry ~ Gen. Marshall will
tell you all about has my heart ~
mind in it. Your people ~ mine
demand the establishment of a front
to draw off pressure on the Russians,
~ these peoples all wise enough
to see that the Russians are today
killing more Germans ~ destroying
more equipment than you & I
put together. Even if full

Harry Hopkins was President Roosevelt's troubleshooter and
personal envoy, and General George C Marshall the Army's Chief
of Staff. In sending these two men to see Churchill in April 1942,
Roosevelt was dispatching two of his very best and brightest.

Success is not attained, the
big objection will be.

So to it =! Syria + Egypt
will be made ^{more} secure, even if
the "Germans" find out about
our plans.

Best of luck — make Harry
go to bed early + let him
obey Dr. Fulton U.S.N. whom
I am sending with him as
super nurse with full
authority

As ever
FDR

ABOVE: Churchill wearing his iconic siren suit in Cairo in 1942, with the British ambassador's baby son and Field Marshal Smuts, Churchill's Boer War opponent but now a firm friend and ally.

OPPOSITE: American Sherman tanks mop up after the British victory at Alamein.

Montgomery of Alamein (1887–1976)

Bernard Montgomery ("Monty"), later Field Marshal Viscount Montgomery of Alamein, was the best known to the wartime public of all Churchill's generals and also probably the most controversial.

Although very influential in his great successes from 1942 onwards, his pre-Alamein career is not so well known. He served in the First World War, during which he was awarded the DSO for his bravery in an action in which he was seriously injured. He then served as a staff officer for some of the biggest battles of that conflict, including the Somme. The generals of the Second World War were the survivors of the carnage of Flanders, and this made an enormous difference to the way in which they conducted their campaigns as commanders.

Montgomery also spent time as an instructor at Staff College, which greatly influenced how he went on later to treat the ordinary soldiers under his command, and his understanding of logistics.

His command of the Third Division in France in 1940 gave him his first taste of real battle. The fact that his troops were able to escape successfully at Dunkirk that year with so few casualties made him one of the British generals to emerge with credit.

There was even a motion of no confidence against Churchill in Parliament – he survived the vote, maintaining the support of most members of the House of Commons, but at the time his position looked briefly perilous as wartime news continued to be grim.

However, now the United States was in the war – the reason Churchill was in Washington DC was to discuss Allied strategy. Chief of Staff George C Marshall's offer of American tanks to be sent immediately to North Africa was happily accepted, and those supplies, along with the superior strategic grasp of General Bernard Montgomery, combined to grant Britain its one unaided victory of the whole conflict, the Second Battle of Alamein in November 1942 (which so enthused Churchill that he ordered church bells to be rung in celebration).

Not only that, but it was now Churchill's concept of how the war ought to be fought rather than that of the American planners that prevailed. He had been anxious that a Japan-first strategy should be followed, while Roosevelt stayed loyal to keeping the defeat of Hitler as the Allied priority. Churchill and his generals had all seen the carnage of the Western Front during the First World War, the thousands butchered on the Somme being uppermost in their minds. The Americans favoured a direct assault on north-west Europe, preferably in 1943 (not, contrary to legend, in 1942, such an assault only being necessary if the Soviet Union looked close to collapse). Churchill and his advisers, such as the new Chief of the Imperial General Staff, the cautious Sir Alan Brooke, opposed this, preferring instead the "peripheral" approach. This method, traditional to Britain since John Churchill's time and even before that, meant attacking the enemy on the edges before going for the main assault.

Britain's dire peril in North Africa actually worked in Churchill's favour: he was able to persuade Roosevelt to countermand the American military and agree to land American troops in North Africa, an operation called "Torch". This appealed to Roosevelt, as it meant that US troops would be operational immediately against Germany, rather than waiting in Britain for a D-Day scheduled for 1943, as Marshall and Eisenhower preferred. However, the American military felt slighted by it, and as the following year progressed and American power became commensurately larger, Churchill's domination of wartime strategy was to prove short-lived.

RIGHT: US troops landing near Oran in November 1942 – symbol of the American contribution for which Churchill had fought so hard.

Churchill and the Grand Alliance

During the war, the three major leaders in the fight against Hitler – Churchill, Roosevelt and Stalin – became known as the "Big Three". However, it was not until late November 1943 that they all finally met, in the Iranian capital Tehran, for a meeting codenamed "Eureka". Apart from one more meeting, at Yalta in 1945, they never met as a group again.

Churchill had wooed Roosevelt from September 1939 onwards, and from the British leader's angle, this courting had proved successful, despite their disagreements on strategy. Their main aim was a victory for the democracies and the defeat of totalitarianism worldwide. Whatever their differences, they remained united on the main goals.

However, in the 1930s, Stalin had been a more brutal dictator than even Hitler, with millions dying in the Soviet purges and in the ruthless collectivization programme in the Ukraine. Not only that, but Stalin was in the war because the Soviet Union had been invaded by its former ally Germany – it was not as if he was on the side of Britain by choice.

By 1943, the fighting between the Red Army and the Wehrmacht had exceeded anything in the war between Germany and the West. Eighty-five per cent of German soldiers killed during the Second World War died on the Eastern Front, with millions of Soviet citizens, mainly civilians, also dying. Stalin continued to press for a "Second Front" against Germany – a British-American invasion through France. But, as Roosevelt's Secretary of State Cordell Hull reported, this was something that Churchill and his advisers feared, as they remembered all too vividly the carnage of the Western Front on which Churchill had himself fought. The repeated postponement of a Second Front was to make Stalin even more paranoid towards the West, and one can see that the later tensions of the Cold War were already germinating in his mind.

From Churchill's point of view, the war was going well. 1943 saw final Allied victory in North Africa and the successful capture of Sicily as a bridgehead for the invasion of the Italian peninsula. However, 1943 was also the last year in which Churchill could feel that Britain's war contribution was as important as that of the United States.

At the first Quebec conference (codenamed "Quadrant") in August 1943, Churchill met together with both Roosevelt and the Canadian Prime Minister Mackenzie King, and, while Churchill had to make concessions to the Americans, he was still able to feel that decisions on how to win were going in the way he felt best. We can describe "Quadrant" as Churchill's last hurrah, both for him personally as a leader of equal stature to his allies, and for Britain as a country in relation to the now overwhelming industrial, logistical and military might of the United States.

Stalin (1878–1953)

Joseph Stalin was the effective ruler of the USSR from Lenin's death in 1924 until his own in 1953, and for most of that period, including wartime, exercised complete dictatorial power.

By 1939, famine and Stalin's purges had killed millions of his own people. Then, in 1939–41, the USSR and Germany were virtually allied, so that Stalin was shocked at the Nazi invasion and took a while to resist effectively. Some 20 million Soviet citizens died during 1941–45.

Stalin was a suspicious ally of the West, and was especially wary of Churchill, whose earlier anti-Bolshevism he did not forget. A ruthless leader of his own people, he used the war to conquer most of Central and Eastern Europe for the Communist cause, crushing Poland in the process.

The West and Stalin were allies in 1941–45, but out of the need to defeat Hitler. That done, the Cold War of 1948–89 was not long in starting.

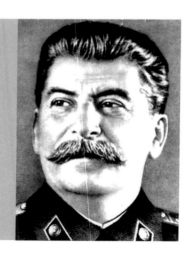

ABOVE: Churchill with Mackenzie King, the Canadian Prime Minister, in August 1943: theirs was not always an easy relationship.

The traditional British way of waging war – on limited resources – and the massive American military concept of hitting the main enemy at their strongest point now came into play, with major results for both the Churchill/Roosevelt relationship and also the group dynamic with the third member of the Big Three, Stalin.

For hundreds of years, Britain had argued for what is called the peripheral approach, attacking the principal enemy sideways on, and

not directly. Not only that, but Britain's real power was at sea, and land wars were always fought with continental allies. This had been the case with Churchill's own great ancestor John Churchill, Duke of Marlborough, against the French – something that the British Prime Minister knew from his multi-volume biography of the Duke and from his own extensive study of history.

The fall of France in 1940 had removed Britain's continental ally, rendering obsolete this centuries-old way of warfare. Britain's new ally the United States was on the other side of an ocean and, more significantly, it was a country many times more powerful than Britain and France put together.

Churchill's traditional British policy, while unquestionably right for the past, was now looking increasingly antiquated. This was an era of global war, fought well beyond the confines of Marlborough's Europe, and beyond the scope of the more limited kind of imperial wars that had been fought against less well-armed enemies (in which Churchill had been engaged as a young man). It was industrial war on an altogether historically unprecedented scale, and not even a historian as well versed as Churchill fully grasped the nature of the change as 1943 unfolded.

Although the invasion of Sicily had gone well, it soon became apparent that Italy was not friendly terrain for invaders from the south. Despite the best efforts of the Allied forces under Eisenhower, with Patton and Montgomery as his subordinates, the capture of the peninsula proved painfully slow going, with victory remaining elusive right down to 1945. And nothing in Italy even began to approach the carnage of the Eastern Front. It is possible to see Stalin's point of view if we compare the figures of two of the key battles of 1942, El Alamein and Stalingrad: British losses at Alamein were around 13,000 killed or injured, while the Soviet equivalent was well over a million, including 40,000 civilian deaths. Stalin felt that the West was allowing the Soviet Union to bleed, while the British and Americans were fighting the Germans not at the heart of the war but at the periphery.

For Stalin and Roosevelt it was becoming obvious that the major victories were being won by the Soviets against the Germans and by the Americans against the Japanese. For Churchill, still conscious of Britain's greatness, this was less obvious. He had hoped to be able to have private time with Roosevelt to coordinate strategy before meeting Stalin. This Roosevelt effectively refused to do, insisting on bringing the Chinese leader Chiang Kai-shek to a brief meeting in Cairo before the two Western leaders flew on to Iran.

In Tehran, Churchill's fears of becoming the junior partner to the United States and the Soviet Union were swiftly realized. As he later told a friend, Violet Bonham-Carter, the daughter of his old colleague Herbert Asquith:

There I sat with the great Russian bear on one side of me, with paws outstretched, and on the other side the great American buffalo, and between the two sat the poor little English donkey, who was the only one who knew the right way home.

ABOVE: Soviet soldiers and a burning T34 tank at Kursk in July 1943: it is regarded as the biggest tank battle in history and it marked a major shift on the Eastern Front.

OPPOSITE: At the same time as Kursk, Allied soldiers (5th Seaforth Highlanders in the picture) were landing in Sicily: the Mediterranean war was at the heart of Churchill's strategy.

Roosevelt had several private sessions with Stalin, from which Churchill was excluded, to the Prime Minister's great hurt and sorrow. The President gave the Soviet leader definite assurance that D-Day would begin in France in summer 1944 – the American way of hitting the enemy directly would now begin, whatever Churchill's fears. The Americans were also now open to compromise on the borders of Poland, the country for which Britain had gone to war in 1939, only for it to be occupied by the Soviets from the east as by the Nazis from the west.

According to his physician, Lord Moran, Churchill left Tehran feeling sad, his "black dog" raging. The Allies were winning, but not in the way that he would have wished.

Churchill Walks Out

Churchill was very perturbed in Tehran that Roosevelt would not lunch alone with him, but would agree to do so with Stalin instead. Several three-way dinners did take place, however, and one of these went very badly. Stalin, whose purges had slaughtered millions, joked tastelessly that after victory, 50,000 Germans should be summarily shot. Roosevelt then quipped that it should be 49,000 instead, a remark endorsed by his son Elliot, who was also a guest. Churchill was outraged at this disregard for civilized rules of war and stormed out in disgust, depressed also that Roosevelt was clearly currying favour with the Soviet dictator. Events were to show that Churchill was right: the Soviets were to execute far more than 50,000 Germans, Russian Cossacks and non-Communist Poles in the months ahead.

D-Day and Beyond

Churchill and his Chief of Imperial General Staff Sir Alan Brooke feared what D-Day might bring. Both lived in terror lest it be a repetition of the first day of the Battle of the Somme, when over 60,000 men from the British army became casualties.

Howeyer, except at the American landing area of Omaha Beach, losses on 6 June 1944 turned out to be well under such gloomy prognostications. Estimates differ, but the very highest figures are around 10,000 killed or injured, with others arguing for a considerably lower figure. Some 175,000 Allied troops were landed on the Normandy beaches, and, lest we forget, many of those were British and Canadian as well as from the United States. Unsurprisingly, Churchill had wanted to accompany the invasion force and observe the troops as they landed on the beaches. This would have been too dangerous, and in the end he had to be persuaded out of it by the King.

A fear that was realized, however, was the inability to keep to Field Marshal Montgomery's optimistic plan of capturing the important city of Caen on the first day. The *bocage*

or patchwork countryside of Normandy proved very difficult for a campaign of movement, and the initial conquest of German-held territory therefore took much longer than at first planned.

D-Day was probably the last major military operation of the war in which the British fought as equals with the United States. Thereafter, the American contribution was inevitably far larger, and as a result the relative importance of the two nations changed considerably, with Britain becoming the junior partner. Churchill was to come to understand this with increasing sorrow as the campaign progressed. Meanwhile, the titanic struggle on the Eastern Front was at all times far larger than anything taking place in north-west Europe, though

this does not in any way minimize the heroism and fighting spirit of the Allies on the Western Front.

Churchill would have preferred a more martial attitude from the British (and American) soldiers nonetheless. One of the major controversies in describing the battles between the Germans and the Allied invaders is the argument that the Wehrmacht fought in a way that produced more casualties – and indeed fanaticism – than conscript soldiers from the Western democracies. Many authors maintain that the Germans consistently outclassed the Western Allies, and that it was the sheer weight of American logistics and industrial production that in the end won the war

for Britain and the United States. The Germans were not so much outfought as outproduced, and on the Eastern Front the key factor, apart from the much-lauded generalship of Marshal Zhukov – whom most historians esteem – was the lack of concern by Stalin for a casualty rate that would have been completely unacceptable in democratic societies.

This may be true, as writers such as Sir Max Hastings have consistently argued for years. Churchill, this theory runs, had the right martial spirit to combat an enemy as uniquely terrible as Nazi Germany. However, the Allied commanders were very aware of the need to avoid the kind of carnage seen in the First World War, and this made a great difference to the way that they saw their troops, as people conscripted to fight and not simply as cannon fodder. And in relation to German forces, British and American troops were from democracies, countries for whom the racial fanaticism of the Third Reich was alien and repugnant.

So, while Allied generals were naturally more cautious than their opponents – with good cause - when it comes to Churchill himself,

ABOVE: British troops on Utah Beach in Normandy, taking up positions just after the first landings on D-Day.

OPPOSITE: Allied ships wait off the coast of Normandy in 1944, ready for great things…

all agree that in him Britain possessed a wartime leader worthy of the country's greatest fighting traditions, a descendant finally equal to his great martial ancestor.

As one of his biographers has put it, from "the summer of 1944 until the end of the war, Churchill was almost constantly on the move". The fact that Churchill was now aged 70 mattered to him not a whit, and he was also able to overcome a major bout of pneumonia, an illness that would have felled many half his age.

We now know that American troops stayed on in Europe after victory and that in 1949 NATO was founded to meet the perceived

threat from the Soviet Union, a threat that Churchill had predicted even during the Second World War.

But at the time no one thought such an outcome likely, and 1944 saw one of Churchill's most controversial moves, his so-called "naughty agreement" or "percentages agreement" with Stalin, in which he and the Soviet dictator carved up Eastern Europe between them, with Greece, for example, being in the British zone of influence,

ABOVE: Churchill and Montgomery touring the Allied beach heads in Normandy shortly after D-Day.

OPPOSITE: Churchill posing with troops in Normandy in July 1944: he had wanted to land with the troops on D-Day but the King and Sir Alan Brooke dissuaded him.

Allied Disagreements Continue

By D-Day, the American vision of how to prosecute the war prevailed, although Churchill's desire to see campaigns in Italy, and, later on, an invasion of Yugoslavia, continued. His major disagreement in 1944 was over Operation "Anvil" (later codenamed "Dragoon"), the Allied invasion of southern France that took place a few weeks after the Normandy landings. Churchill, still wedded to a Mediterranean strategy, was worried at the numbers of troops that would have to be transferred out of Italy, and was also unimpressed by the arguments for "Anvil". But by this stage of the war his comparative power in relation to the United States had diminished, and he was unable to prevail, either in keeping Italy as important as he would have liked or in preventing "Anvil" from taking place as the Americans wished.

Yugoslavia divided 50/50 and states such as Bulgaria predominantly in the Soviet sphere. (Poland was still up for discussion, an issue dealt with later at Yalta in 1945.)

This was controversial both at the time and later on. Some have accused Churchill of appeasing Stalin in a way that was no different from the way in which Chamberlain similarly sought to appease Hitler before 1939, and outwardly such an argument has some force. But one can also say that Churchill was being realistic given the facts as he saw them at the time, with the United States out of the picture and a seriously war-weakened Britain having to stand alone against the might of a victorious Soviet Union.

And in fact one can say that Churchill was also successful. Greece stayed in the Western camp, later to become a member of both NATO and, after Churchill's death, the European Union. Yugoslavia was able, in 1948, to withdraw from the Soviet zone without any attempt by Stalin to invade that country and to force it back to obedience in the way that Hungary was crushed in 1956. Stalin, unlike Hitler at Munich in 1938, kept his word to Churchill.

On D-Day much hope existed of the war finishing by the end of the year. But the delays in Normandy, and then the debacle at Arnhem – the "bridge too far" – along with the continued resilience of the German army, all conspired together to prevent an Allied victory as soon as Churchill and others had hoped. The war would have several more months to run.

ABOVE: The British authors of victory – Churchill with Field Marshals Montgomery and Brooke (later Alanbrooke) inspecting tank traps in France in 1944.

BELOW: Churchill on a flying visit to Normandy in August 1944 – being introduced to one of Montgomery's puppies!

OPPOSITE: Churchill's relationship with De Gaulle was uneasy but in November 1944 they could celebrate Armistice Day happily in Paris.

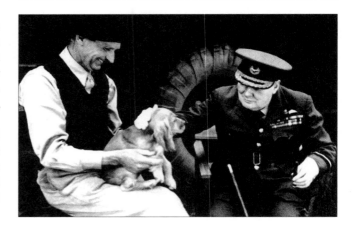

Triumph and Tragedy

The year 1945 saw the end of the costliest war in history, with over 55 million killed globally. As Churchill feared, much of the world was saved not for democracy but for another kind of tyranny, albeit one based on ideology rather than on race.

In February came the last meeting of the Big Three, in the Soviet resort town of Yalta in the Crimea. By this time, as Churchill had grasped, Britain's role in the post-war world was distinctly junior to that of the United States and the Soviet Union. However, he made the best of it, paying generous tribute to Stalin's role, even though he and the Soviet dictator disagreed strongly on how a post-war Europe should be run. Russian tanks might have overrun Poland, but Churchill did his utmost to ensure – sadly in vain – that some small vestige of genuine Polish democracy would be allowed. The post-1945 map of Europe was effectively determined at Yalta, with Churchill's main achievement being to secure an occupation zone for France in Germany, alongside the American, British and Soviet zones.

By this time the British and Americans had regained the momentum lost in the Ardennes and the Battle of the Bulge. In March

the Allies were finally able to make the crossing of the Rhine, and on Churchill's first visit on 23 March he symbolically urinated into the river, a physical demonstration of his contempt for his enemies that he deemed "most satisfactory"! On 25 March, Churchill came close to being shelled, and might have been killed but for the prescience of the American commander General William Simpson, who took him away just in time, much to Field Marshal Alan Brooke's relief.

Churchill, ever mindful of the fate of post-war Europe, hoped that the Western Allies would make a military push and capture Berlin. In this he was thwarted both by Eisenhower's decision to keep to the Yalta agreements with Stalin and by Marshall's decision that the fighting should be based upon military, not political, targets. In addition, General Omar Bradley felt that the United States could lose up to 100,000 men in the attempt, too high a sacrifice with

ABOVE: The three leaders and their aides at the Livadia Palace, Yalta, February 1945. Seated, left to right: Churchill, Roosevelt, Stalin.

OPPOSITE: Churchill and Brooke crossing the River Rhine on the back of a tank.

Why Tragedy as Well as Triumph?

In Churchill's *The Second World War*, the final volume is entitled *Triumph and Tragedy*. His choice of title may seem odd, given the triumph of the victorious Allies. Yet Churchill was right to see tragedy as well as triumph, in ways that are only now seeping into the popular understanding of the Second World War.

First, who won the war? Certainly the old British ditty "we won the war in 1944" may reflect common sentiment but in reality it is entirely untrue. As Churchill fully realized, for all its successes on D-Day, Britain was now a minnow in comparison with the United States and the Soviet Union. One can argue that in effect the Soviet Union won the war against Germany and the United States that against Japan. For a patriot as profound as Churchill, Britain's comparative loss of status was a bitter blow, even if his country was on the winning side.

Second, the large amount of space that Churchill devotes to the Polish issue in the book shows that he understood, even in 1944–45, what it took until after 1989 for many Westerners to grasp – namely that the end of the war was a complete disaster for millions of Central Europeans, such as the Poles, since they were in effect simply substituting one alien dictatorship for another, Soviet instead of Nazi. In the West we think of the conflict as being a "good war": that was not the case for Poland, Czechoslovakia and other countries who had to suffer over four decades of often brutal Soviet occupation. Freedom for them did not come until 1989, 24 years after Churchill's death.

ABOVE: An iconic picture – Russian soldiers flying the Red Flag over the ruins of the Reichstag in Berlin, 30 April 1945. Churchill had hoped the Western Allies would arrive in Berlin first.

LEFT: Massive rejoicing – people dancing in a London street on VE Day, May 1945.

OPPOSITE, TOP: Churchill greeting the exultant crowds from the balcony of Buckingham Palace with King George VI and his family.

OPPOSITE, BOTTOM: Churchill giving an election speech during the 1945 general election. The war had been fought with a coalition government and he was soon to lose power.

war against Japan then thought to entail even higher losses. The numerous Red Army casualties in the struggle for Berlin proved Bradley's point, but that should not blind us to the fact that politically speaking Churchill's fear of post-victory tensions between the West and the Soviet Union were to be swiftly vindicated.

VE (Victory in Europe) Day came on 8 May 1945, and the enthusiastic crowds in London cheered Churchill loudly as he appeared triumphantly on the balcony of Buckingham Palace along with the royal family. His critics may be right to say that victory had come at a cost, but we should not forget that in 1940 so glorious a conclusion had seemed almost impossible. By the time that VJ Day – victory over Japan – came on 15 August 1945 (2 September in the United States), however, Churchill was out of office.

Was the cost to Britain and its empire worth it? Britain was now bankrupt, and as for the Empire, in which Churchill so much believed, that too soon would pass, with India becoming independent by 1947. But surely the alternative was defeat? Could Britain ever have won without the United States, as the revisionists claim? Surely not must be the correct answer, and the rise to superpower status for the United States was equally inevitable. How high is the price of

Nº 52370

ALLIED
EXPEDITIONARY FORCE
PERMIT

The bearer of this permit has the permission
of the Supreme Commander Allied Expeditionary
Force to enter the Zone of the Allied Forces in

Le titulaire est autorisé d'entrer dans la Zone
de l'Armée Alliée en

N.W. EUROPE.

This permit must be produced when required
together with the bearer's identity document.
Ce permis doit être présenté à toute demande
avec le document d'identité du titulaire.

The Allies had finally won the war and Churchill was now exploring the conquered Germany, en route to meeting Truman and Stalin at Potsdam. But British democracy had just spoken – he was soon to be voted out of office now that VE Day was over, in favour of Clement Attlee and a Labour government.

MILITARY PERMIT OFFICE

Issued by } LONDON
Emis par }
Date .... 4 JUL 1945

Valid from } 4 JUL 1945 until } 4 OCT 1945
Validité du } au }
Destination: AEF OP AREA including GERMANY.

Object of } OFFICIAL DUTY
Journey }
Occupation... PRIME MINISTER AND MINISTER OF DEFENCE

Full name of } THE RIGHT HON:
Bearer } WINSTON LEONARD
Prénom et nom } SPENCER CHURCHILL
du Titulaire } P.C. C.H. M.P.

Nationality } BRITISH
Nationalité }

Number and Type of } BRIT. P.V. Nº 7359
Identity Document }

Ministry or Dept. } FOREIGN OFFICE
supporting journey }

Signature { of Bearer
{ du Titulaire } ....

....
...

Issuing Officer's Signature, Rank and Appointment

For Supreme Commander, A.E.F.

Endorsements

Holder has permission to retain this Permit for repeated journeys within the dates of validity

Military Permit Officer

(B44/618) 35000 10/44 W.O.P. 19372

freedom and the defeat of an evil as monstrous as Nazism? Whatever some historians say – however well-meaning – it must be that a balanced view of the war leads us to conclude that when Churchill declared in 1940 that victory "whatever the cost" was the only option, he was incontestably right. And since it was his "Great Republic", his mother's country the United States, that was the new defender of democracy, that too was an outcome to be applauded.

It seems extraordinary that Churchill was rejected by the electorate in the general election of 1945 that followed victory in Europe. But in a sense the British people were distinguishing between Churchill as war leader, for which no praise could be too high, and Churchill as leader of the Conservative Party. It was this party's political programme that the electorate, with its memories of the 1930s, now emphatically rejected. While the results were a major surprise to Churchill and to the wider world, we need to remember that gratitude for salvation in war did not mean endorsement of the Conservative view of post-victory Britain.

RIGHT: Churchill with Montgomery after British troops had entered Germany – in Julich, March 1945.

BELOW: Churchill in Berlin for the Potsdam conference in July 1945: he took a rest on Hitler's chair outside the ruins of the Berlin bunker.

5

STATESMAN

Iron Curtain

Churchill might be out of office, but he was not without influence. In many ways, his official job as Leader of the Opposition was the least important of his roles. But as a result of Allied victory, coupled with Roosevelt's death and an inexperienced President now in the White House, he was the leading statesman of the democratic world.

O n 5 March 1946, Churchill was the guest of President Harry Truman in the President's home state of Missouri. At Westminster College, in the small town of Fulton, he gave an address officially designated as "The Sinews of Peace" but which has gone down in history as his "Iron Curtain" oration. The speech gave recognition to the Cold War that now existed between Britain, the United States and other powers of the Western world on the one hand and their former Soviet wartime ally on the other. Strictly speaking, Churchill did not invent the phrase "Iron Curtain" – the "curtain" was in any case made more of concrete and barbed wire than iron – but the phrase stuck thanks to him, and defined the history of the next four decades between the democratic West and the Communist East. The following is the most famous passage from Churchill's address:

From Stettin in the Baltic to Trieste in the Adriatic an iron curtain has descended across the Continent. Behind that line lie all the capitals of the ancient states of Central and Eastern Europe. Warsaw, Berlin, Prague, Vienna, Budapest, Belgrade, Bucharest and Sofia; all these famous cities and the populations around them lie in what I must call the Soviet sphere, and all are subject in one form or another, not only to Soviet influence but to a very high and, in some cases, increasing measure of control from Moscow.

RIGHT: Churchill and President Truman in Fulton, Missouri in 1946, where he made his famous "Iron Curtain" speech that helped define the Cold War.

However, Churchill's speech was equally about the importance of relations between Britain and the United States – Churchill's "English-Speaking Peoples" idea – that was at the heart of how he saw the post-war world emerging. Churchill viewed Britain uniquely as being at the centre of three interlocking circles: United States–Britain, Britain–Europe and Britain–Commonwealth. This could be said to be his leitmotif, and an issue that has dogged British politics ever since: is Britain principally a European country or closer to the United States across the Atlantic? Churchill greatly encouraged the ravaged nations of wartime Europe to become closer to one another and to coexist in peace. But he also made clear that he would not take Britain down, as he saw it, to the level of Belgium. Indian Independence in 1947 was an act he could not undo, but to Churchill the British Empire remained vital to his country's global prestige, as did the enormous outlay of military strength that did not diminish until after his death.

Even in the twenty-first century, the issue that dominated Churchill's strategic thinking – that Britain is a country which punches above its weight internationally and preferably in tandem with the United States – remains at the heart of the nation's debate.

In March 1946, as Churchill correctly pointed out, Czechoslovakia was still a democracy. But, as he foresaw, that would not be for long, and in 1948 the Communist coup in Prague condemned that nation to 41 years of Soviet rule. Historians differ on when exactly the Cold War began and argue about which key event triggered it. However, in understanding the issues as clearly as he did in Fulton, Churchill prophetically grasped the dominant strategic/ideological issue of his time and indeed of the world right down until the collapse of the Soviet Union in 1991, a full 26 years after his death.

ABOVE LEFT: At an 8th Army reunion in 1946 – Churchill was now Leader of the Opposition and out of power but still revered.

ABOVE RIGHT: Churchill delivering the actual speech in Fulton, at Westminster College, which has a library devoted to him.

Churchill and Europe

In the 2010 general election, 45 years after his death, Winston Churchill was still appearing on election posters. However, the posters were not for his Conservative Party but for UKIP (UK Independence Party), a party founded well after his lifetime. Churchill remains as politically iconic now as he was in the last quarter of his life, and significantly with regard to the debate over Europe. All sides claim Churchill, but perhaps Churchill's other famous post-war speech, made in Zurich on 19 September 1946, provides his authentic view:

The first step is to form a Council of Europe... In all this urgent work, France and Germany must take the lead together. Great Britain, the British Commonwealth of nations, mighty America and I trust Soviet Russia... must be friends of the new Europe and must champion its right to live and shine.

Churchill favoured European unity, but with Britain benignly on the outside. Whether he was right is as politically contentious today as ever – his sons-in-law were strong supporters of British involvement in Europe – but his own views, mistaken or prophetic, are clear.

WESTMINSTER COLLEGE

CHARTERED IN 1853

FULTON, MISSOURI

October 3, 1945

The Honorable Winston Churchill, M. P.
London
England

My dear Mr. Churchill:

In 1936 an English-born woman, Mrs. John Findley Green, established at Westminster College a memorial lectureship to be known as the John Findley Green Foundation. The lectureship was established to bring to the college campus each year a man of international reputation who would discuss economic, social, or political problems of international concern in a series of three or four lectures. After the lectures are delivered, the lecturer leaves the manuscript with the college in order that they may be published in book form.

This letter is to invite you to deliver the Green Lectures in the winter of 1945-1946, or in the spring of 1946. We should be glad to arrange the date or dates to suit your convenience.

The arrangement for the scheduling of the lectures may be made to suit your convenience. It had been our thought to have one lecture at the college one evening and to have another lecture delivered in St. Louis, Missouri (U.S.A.) on the evening of the following day. The college is located one hundred miles from this metropolitan center and we should like to arrange for your appearance under the auspices of the Green Foundation before the great audience which would assemble in St. Louis to hear you. We know that any discussions coming from you and delivered from this forum here in the heart of the United States will be of immense and enduring significance, and will promote the international understanding requisite to the maintenance of peace. We earnestly hope that you will do us the honor of accepting this invitation.

A suitable honorarium will be provided. In this instance, we shall also be glad to allow you to arrange for the publication of the lectures, or we shall make the arrangement and allow you to share in the royalties.

Enclosed you will find excerpt from the Instrument of Gift, establishing the John Findley Green Foundation Lectureship at Westminster College.

This is a wonderful school in my home state. Hope you can do it. I'll introduce you. Best regards

Harry Truman

Yours respectfully,

F. L. McCluer
President

FLM:D
enclosure (1)

Churchill was one of the very few Western statesmen who realised that the alliance with the USSR could not last. His speech in Fulton, Missouri, was to set the scene for the next forty years and prove Churchill to be prophetic. The invitation from the University was accompanied by a personal one from President Truman, with a note in his own hand added to the official invite.

Indian Summer

In 1951, just before his seventy-seventh birthday, Churchill became Prime Minister for the second time, now head of a peacetime Conservative government. Some (including perhaps Clementine) wished he had retired in 1945, his mission to save his country accomplished, with no post-war partisan reputation to lessen his image.

But while his "Indian Summer" administration of 1951–55 did not achieve the great dreams that he had held for it, notably a conference that would lead to peace with the Soviet Union, it was certainly no failure. And given that Churchill's successor Anthony Eden turned out to be as unlucky as Churchill had feared, especially in his handling of the Suez Crisis, there is much to be said for the view that Churchill was better qualified than anyone else in the Conservative Party to be its leader and Prime Minister.

In any case, his administration was not altogether partisan. He offered posts to Liberals, which they declined, and he repealed amazingly few of the changes of the Labour government of 1945–51. The National Health Service remained fully intact, coal stayed nationalized (though the steel industry was privatized) and much of the post-war consensus continued even though the Labour Party was now in opposition. Although it is often right-wing Conservatives who claim Churchill today, his government in fact changed very little domestically, and in the record amount of houses built for ordinary people – thanks to the enthusiasm of Harold Macmillan – the One Nation brand of moderate Conservatism came very much to the fore. In appointing Sir Walter Monckton as Minister of Labour and National Service, Churchill had chosen someone calculated not to annoy the trade unions rather than to reform or antagonize them.

Inevitably it was on the issues of foreign affairs and defence that Churchill concentrated most. After again fulfilling the role of Defence Minister himself for a brief time, he gave this post to the non-political Second World War commander Field Marshal Alexander in the House of Lords, which meant that Churchill effectively remained in control. With regard to foreign policy too – much to the fury of his Foreign Secretary, Anthony Eden – Churchill tried all possible means to keep charge, with initiatives of his own sometimes put forward without the knowledge either of Eden or indeed of Britain's close allies.

He kept to the policy of encouraging European unity – but from the outside: Britain did not join the European Coal and Steel Community. Churchill's closest tie remained with the United States, especially after his old wartime colleague Dwight Eisenhower became President in January 1953. Eisenhower in fact favoured

Britain becoming more closely integrated into Europe, and had done so when he was briefly Supreme Allied Commander of the new NATO. But he felt that Churchill was a great man, if past his prime, and was as kind as possible outwardly, meeting up with him, for example, in Bermuda in late 1953, and taking some of Churchill's ideas for his own Atoms for Peace proposal to the United Nations. Just seeing Eisenhower brought much-needed vigour back to an increasingly frail Churchill, as well as happy memories of earlier days.

For Churchill the "special relationship" between the United States and Britain remained at the heart of British foreign and defence policy, more vital than Europe or the Commonwealth. But he was perhaps the last Prime Minister under whom Britain could be thought of as an equal to the United States, and when, in 1956, Eisenhower forced a drastic change in British policy at Suez

Printed by Maysigns, 142, High Street North, East Ham, E.6. and published by
Col. W. H. Barlow-Wheeler, 14, Grove Crescent, South Woodford, E.18.

Churchill's physical appearance and his iconic cigars became
so well known that a 1950s election poster could simply
put him and one of them in silhouette and everyone would
recognize him instantly.

PAGE 140: Churchill and President Eisenhower in Washington DC in 1954 – the balance of power between the two men very different from wartime.

LEFT: Churchill escorts Queen Elizabeth II to her car after dining at 10 Downing St, April 1955.

ABOVE: City businessmen read a newspaper announcing Churchill's final retirement in April 1955.

BELOW: Eden watches Churchill addressing the Conservative Party Conference in 1953.

Anthony Eden (1897–1977, 1ˢᵗ Earl of Avon)

It was always said of Eden that he was like a favourite for the Derby, primed to win in 1938 but not let out of the stables until too late in 1955. Eden is now remembered unfavourably, because of the Suez Crisis in October 1956, yet it was not supposed to have been that way. A decorated veteran of the First World War, he was originally the glamorous and great future hope of the Conservative Party, becoming Foreign Secretary for the first time aged only 38 in 1935. He was widely deemed to have been anti-appeasement and resigned in protest over this policy in February 1938, to great acclaim from Churchill.

But his two subsequent outings as Foreign Secretary were under Churchill, a leader who really did understand foreign policy and was strongly inclined to follow his own inclinations, often to Eden's despair. One of the few independent decisions Eden made, to send troops to rescue Greece in 1941, ended in military disaster. Throughout this period Eden was *de facto* deputy, and therefore spent 15 years as the heir in waiting, finally becoming Prime Minister in 1955 when Churchill retired. He survived Churchill by nearly 12 years and, unlike his predecessor, is increasingly forgotten, an impatient crown prince who could never really – as Churchill had suspected – wear the crown himself.

Telephone
Lambourn 48.

May 15th 1952

The Right Hon Winston Churchill.

Dear Sir.

Thank you very much indeed for the present I received for dead-Heating on "Pol Roger" at Liverpool.

I only wish I could have won outright for you.

Yours Sincerely

Lester Piggott.

ABOVE: Churchill loved riding and the horses in general – it is significant too that he named his horse after his favourite drink Pol Roger. Lester Piggott was soon to become Britain's most famous jockey, but did not alas win this time for Churchill in 1952.

– just a year after Churchill's retirement – the uneven nature of the relationship became clear.

For the coronation of Queen Elizabeth II in 1953, the young Queen made Churchill a Knight of the Garter, so he became Sir Winston. (He refused a dukedom, remaining the "great commoner".) Churchill had a grandfatherly relationship with Elizabeth, rather like that Lord Melbourne had enjoyed with the equally youthful Queen Victoria over a century earlier.

In June 1953, soon after the coronation, Churchill had a major stroke, which incapacitated him for months. In that more deferential age, the true extent of his illness could be concealed, and he was able to recover in tranquillity and privacy. But by April 1955 he felt that he really did need to retire, and he did so in style, the Queen coming to dine with him at 10 Downing Street.

Churchill's political career had come to an end but his influence behind the scenes continued – for example he was consulted about who should succeed Eden as Prime Minister in 1957 after the Suez debacle. Technically he remained an MP until 1964, though his appearances in the House of Commons became rarer as his health deteriorated and he spent more time abroad. His last years were marred by strokes, and general ill-health. But as an icon of Britain at its greatest, he retained his "national treasure" status right to the end.

The Great Orator

Churchill always hoped to win the Nobel Peace Prize, though it is fair to say that he would have done all possible in the 1950s to prevent nuclear war regardless of that wish. But he was awarded a Nobel Prize: for literature. Part of this was in recognition of his unique oratory, perhaps unmatched by any other statesman in the past century. The other reason though was for his extraordinary literary output, which put his achievements well above other politicians since the nineteenth century (who today reads Disraeli's novels or Gladstone's commentaries?).

Churchill's oratory in 1940 was magnificent, and even today it is hard to read his speeches without feeling profoundly moved. Strictly speaking, it was planned oratory, or to be more precise, rhetoric, although the electrifying effect on the listener is the same. Very few of Churchill's famous orations were spontaneous. The Churchill Archives contain his original drafts, and many speeches were written and then rewritten numerous times. They were then typed out by his secretaries in what is called "psalm form", a way of transcribing words so that they appear not in normal paragraphs but with the emphases placed on particular words. The care Churchill took over his oratory was enormous, and he felt that his speeches to the House of Commons – designed to persuade his audience by promoting debate and discussion – were at the heart of the democratic process. Far more than being just for show, his rhetoric was an attempt to win his fellow Britons to whatever cause he was advocating at the time. During the war, that cause was the very survival of civilization itself.

However, it was ordinary citizens outside Parliament who were the most swayed by Churchill's oratory. Live broadcasting did not come until after Churchill's death, but people listened to repeats of the speeches broadcast by the BBC. Indeed one of the most iconic pictures from that time is of people gathered around a large radio in a public place like a pub, or in a private home, eagerly listening to the great man speaking as if he were with them in person.

Today, in a television age of sound bites, oratory sadly seems to have no place. Two-minute extracts on the news make even the greatest of Churchill's wartime speeches seem overlong. But those speeches certainly inspired a whole generation of people around the world, and they have stood the test of time as literature in their own right. If we do not hear such words today, we are the poorer for it.

OPPOSITE: Iconic *Picture Post* photos of drinkers in a pub listening to one of Churchill's famous wartime speeches in 1941.

LEFT: A young Churchill makes a speech to women at the Cambridge Hall, Wanstead, 10 October 1924.

BELOW: Characteristic shots of Churchill making a speech in Ottawa, Canada in 1952: still able to weave his oratorical spell.

The Writing of Churchill's Later Books

Churchill's later works, the volumes that made up *A History of the English-Speaking Peoples* and *The Second World War*, were all essentially joint efforts. Unlike many "celebrities" who use ghostwriters today, Churchill was always completely open about the fact that he wrote with assistance, with many of his team having considerable specialist knowledge in their own right. These specialists used material that Churchill had written, such as memoranda or telegrams, weaving them into a literary tapestry to which he then added his own thoughts and reflections. The works may have been compiled by a "syndicate", but the words are Churchill's.

The Twilight Years

After his retirement from frontline politics in 1955, Churchill spent much of his time travelling. He returned to locations he had known in his younger years and revisited some places he had discovered during the war. The South of France was his destination of choice for much of this time, and he and Clementine spent many happy vacations there.

It was the English who made the South of France famous as a holiday destination in the early nineteenth century, and so it is fitting that Churchill – who embodied so many of Britain's best values – regarded it as his favourite haunt for most of his adult life, and increasingly so after 1955. Many of his paintings were set there, and it had long been for him a place of refuge in testing times, most notably, for example, after losing office in 1945.

By the 1950s, Churchill was the most famous man in the world and it was a considerable honour to be his host. The rich and not quite so famous vied with each other to have the Churchills to stay. As Geoffrey Best has pointed out, with the couple came not only an extraordinary amount of luggage – over 100 suitcases for just one holiday jaunt – but also a vast retinue of valets, bodyguards, private secretaries, research assistants and various members of the family with some time to spare. Churchill liked to be pampered – a lifelong characteristic – and by this time of his life, there was probably a feeling that, having done all he had to save democracy, he deserved it. In addition, absolute privacy was necessary even in a day before the curse of the paparazzi became a hazard. To accommodate all of this, the host needed to be truly rich.

Churchill's occasional host Somerset Maugham was a famous writer in his own right, and various other friends also had villas in the South of France, such as Lord Beaverbrook, the Canadian press tycoon. One of Churchill's hosts was the intellectual Emery Reves. A publisher and literary agent, Reves had helped Churchill with the overseas rights to *The Second World War* and had so been able to arrange the publication that Churchill was legitimately able to avoid

the punitive post-war rates of income tax of the Attlee government – and put aside a nest egg for future generations of the family. Reves was able to perform similar miracles for Churchill's *A History of the English Speaking Peoples* and these deals removed financial worry for Churchill for probably the first time in his life.

It was in the Reveses' sumptuous villa that Churchill first met the most notorious of his millionaire hosts. This was the shipping

OPPOSITE: Winston and Clementine off to the South of France, one of their favourite destinations, September 1952.

BELOW: Churchill in retirement: at the Riviera villa of novelist Somerset Maugham in 1959.

magnate Aristotle Onassis, one of the wealthiest of the generation of Greek shipping-fleet owners who became internationally famous after the war. At the time Onassis was also known as the lover of the opera singer Maria Callas, and it could be said that he collected illustrious politicians, since he also befriended the Kennedy family during this time. Onassis was later infamous for his marriage to the widowed Jacqueline Kennedy some years after Churchill's death. As a guest on one of Onassis's vessels, it was not just a question of cruising around the usual Mediterranean hotspots – one of his voyages went as far as the United States, although Churchill was alas too unwell to disembark when they arrived there.

For someone who was so fond of the United States, Churchill went there little in his later years. But he did manage a final visit in 1959 and, with Eisenhower still in the White House, there was a link with the glorious years of the past. However, when Churchill was made an honorary citizen of the United States by a grateful President Kennedy in 1963, Randolph had to accept the honour on his father's behalf. By this time Churchill's health was often frail but he remained indomitable, supported by his family and respected by the press.

RIGHT: Churchill painting in 1959 in Marrakech, a place he had loved since wartime meetings there.

BELOW: Churchill with one of his controversial hosts of later life, the Greek shipping tycoon Aristotle Onassis.

Protecting Churchill ————————————————

As Churchill's distant cousin Princess Diana was to discover, being famous has its perils as well as its perks. Few people can have been more famous than Winston Churchill. His final years came during a decade that saw the birth of celebrity photography and the pursuit of the iconic image. While the subjects of such photography were usually models, film stars and other members of the *dolce vita*, no one was perhaps more iconic – and in his case deservedly so – than Winston Churchill.

Yet these years also marked his slow physical and mental decline, and safeguarding his privacy became more important than ever. Above all, his family wanted to protect his dignity as old age and senility took their toll. Travel enabled Churchill to escape the public gaze – his hosts such as Lord Beaverbrook and Emery Reves allowed him to take cover behind their villa walls, well away from prying eyes. This was even more the case on yachts such as those owned by Aristotle Onassis – the kind of aerial photography so loved by the media today was not so feasible then.

Churchill College, Cambridge

Churchill was a graduate of the Royal Military Academy at Sandhurst, one of the few recent Prime Ministers not to have attended Oxford, Cambridge or Edinburgh universities. Nevertheless, there is a college named after him at Cambridge. Its foundation reflects the fact that he was one of the most technologically minded Prime Ministers in British history, despite not having any degree, let alone one in science.

He is rightly famed as an enthusiastic supporter of technical innovation, from the tank through to the Mulberry Harbours of the Second World War. Thanks to his Oxford-based scientific adviser Frederick Lindemann (Lord Cherwell), he was at the cutting edge of achievement in this area. But Churchill realized that Britain was woefully behind the United States in terms of technological education, a fact that became clear after he visited the

famous Massachusetts Institute of Technology in 1949.

He felt that Britain needed a similar institution. In 1955, shortly after his retirement as Prime Minister, he was on holiday in Sicily with both Lord Cherwell and Jock Colville, his former Principal Private Secretary. Churchill re-expressed his desire to see the founding of an institution for technology, and Colville set to work, only for them to discover that a group of top British businessmen had been harbouring

as well as from the Transport and General Workers' Union and some major American charitable foundations. Thousands of ordinary individuals also contributed.

A site was found in 1959. The college's design was as deliberately modern as possible and Churchill commemorated the first dig by planting a tree. As he put it to the assembled crowd:

Since we have neither the massive population nor the raw materials, nor yet adequate agricultural land to enable us to make our way in the world with ease, we must depend for survival on our brains, on skilled minds that are at least proportionately equal to those in the United States and Soviet Russia. This is far from being achieved, and even when it is, we shall only have reached a quantitative target. In equality, we should endeavour to outstrip our friends and our rivals as we have done in the past.

similar ambitions for several years. A third group was also working on plans: this was at Colville's old university, Cambridge, and was led by Alexander (later Lord) Todd, the Nobel Prize-winning chemist. Todd was working alongside Carl Gilbert, the American chairman of the Gillette Company (famous for its shaving razor).

Eventually these groups coalesced, with an announcement made in 1958 that a college would be founded at Cambridge. The original plan was to admit graduates only, but while Oxford had two such colleges, Cambridge had none, so the decision was made that undergraduates would be admitted too. At least two-thirds of the students had to be in the sciences, and an appeal for funding was launched, with donations coming mainly from British companies,

Churchill College opened for its first students in 1960, and was given a formal royal charter in August that year. It has since remained true to its founding principles, with approximately 70 percent of its students scientists. The college's motto is "Forward" – a nice reflection of the last sentence of Churchill's famous "Blood, Toil, Tears and Sweat" speech, which he concluded with "Come, then, let us go forward together". For over half a century, the motto has been an inspiration to Churchill College students.

A Glorious Ending

State funerals are normally reserved for monarchs. However, Winston Churchill was no ordinary person and, when he died in 1965, he was accorded a full state funeral given to precious few other commoners over the centuries.

Admiral Horatio Lord Nelson was granted one in 1806, as was Arthur Wellesley, 1st Duke of Wellington, in 1852. One of the greatest British Prime Ministers, William Gladstone, had a state funeral in 1898; his predecessor Benjamin Disraeli was offered one but turned down the option.

Churchill died on 24 January 1965, exactly 70 years after his father's sad death back in 1895. He had suffered from a massive stroke some days earlier, but this time, instead of lingering on in even greater senility, he finally gave out, the suffering and indignity of his last few years now thankfully over.

The Churchill biographer and archivist Piers Brendon is surely right to say that Churchill's state funeral was the grandest awarded to a commoner since Wellington's over a century before, which is perhaps appropriate: Wellington had saved Britain from Napoleon as Churchill had saved Britain from Hitler. Over 320,000 people filed past Churchill's coffin in the medieval splendour of Westminster Hall. Mounted on a great catafalque and guarded by officers from the Queen's own personal bodyguard, it was a spectacle not to be forgotten.

OPPOSITE: Winston Churchill looking out of the window of his London home with Clementine and his nurse in January 1965. This would be the last public glimpse of Churchill.

BELOW: The wreath sent by Her Majesty Queen Elizabeth II. Her message reads: "From the Nation and the Commonwealth in grateful remembrance. Elizabeth R."

Churchill was perhaps the last illustrious Victorian but his funeral was held in an age of television, and the ceremony was beamed around the world. President Lyndon B Johnson may have boycotted the funeral – he sent his Vice-President, Hubert Humphrey – because of the British Prime Minister Harold Wilson's refusal to get involved in Vietnam, but millions of American viewers eagerly watched the ceremony on television. As even the French President Charles de Gaulle – who did attend – had to admit, pomp and circumstance was something that the British did superbly well.

A memorial service was held in Westminster Abbey. It was attended by those of Churchill's great contemporaries still alive, such as Field Marshal Bernard Montgomery and the wartime Deputy Prime Minister Clement Attlee who had succeeded Churchill in Downing Street. Representative soldiers from his old regiments carried the coffin, and thousands lined the streets in London to watch the procession.

Churchill chose not to be buried in Westminster Abbey, though he is commemorated there. Rather he was interred in the churchyard at Bladon not far from his ancestral home at Blenheim. Rather touchingly, when the barge bearing his coffin made its slow way down the River Thames, the large cranes in the riverside warehouses were lowered in a mechanical half-mast – British flags had been flown half-mast around the country during the period of mourning.

In a sense, Churchill's funeral was not just for a man. Countless commentators have written in the decades since that it marked the passing of an era, one in which a British leader could command the world stage as the equal of those of larger and more important countries. In that regard it was not just Churchill's funeral but also of the age in which Britain and its empire had bestrode the world like a colossus. Churchill was the end of that line and, like the man himself, his funeral was iconic.

RIGHT: The cortege at the state funeral of Sir Winston Churchill makes its way down London's Whitehall, with Big Ben symbolically in the background, 30 January 1965.

Churchill and History

One of Churchill's most famous aphorisms is that history would be kind to him because he would write it. Probably more books have been written about Winston Churchill than any other person in British history – nearly half a century after his death, volumes still appear as on no one else, except perhaps his great wartime adversary Adolf Hitler. For certain, no British contemporaries have received such minute treatment.

Churchill is perhaps even more revered in the United States than he is in Britain. Churchill societies abound, and as far as his iconic status is concerned, Americans ensure that the flame blazes on.

Some historians represent the *zeitgeist* of the era in which they live, while others make a reputation by deliberately going against it. Reputations are made in creating heroes and in denigrating them, and the study of Winston Churchill in the decades since he died has proved no exception to this rule of what is sometimes called historiography, the study of how history is written.

Churchill himself certainly believed that history has a theme: that the past cannot be looked at in isolation, and that the contemplation of eras gone by allows us to better understand both our present and how to act in the future. It is perhaps appropriate that the story of how Churchill's biographers have handled him is proof that both history and biography tell one as much about the time in which the books were written, and about the views and ideology of the author, as they do about the subject itself.

We can divide the study of Churchill into three parts. First came the "heroic" stage, in which Churchill's own interpretation of himself played the pivotal role: Churchill was right and his enemies wrong, and all that he did was on the grandest scale.

This was followed by the "revisionist" era, in which historians and biographers, from both the political left and right, used Churchill as a peg upon which to hang important ideological points about the interpretation of British history: Churchill was often wrong, and sometimes disastrously so, in suppressing workers, propagating imperialism or letting the United States become the predominant superpower when in 1940 he decided to fight on rather than cut a peace deal with Hitler.

Thirdly, during the "post-revisionist" or consolidation phase, those writing several decades after Churchill's death are able to put his life into a larger historical perspective. Distance brings with it greater understanding (for example, the collapse of the Soviet Union and the Cold War in 1991 changed the way we look at the world very considerably). Many believe that Churchill was right about all

the important things, especially in opposing Hitler, and it is perfectly possible to be a hero and to make mistakes at the same time.

Churchill could never have expected that his canonical interpretation of the Second World War would be challenged within a very few years of his death. When he wrote his account, heavy restrictions allowed only a very few to see government papers, and none could be seen within 50 years of their being written. However, not long after Churchill died, the government not only changed that 50 years to 30 but also declared that almost all war papers could be viewed (except a very few concerned with secret intelligence, most of which still remain closed).

Historians were now able to discover whether or not Churchill's writings were accurate. It was soon apparent that, like most politicians and memoirists, he had put his own slant and interpretation upon events. Not only that, but because he was in office until 1955, he had been obliged to constrain himself with regard to wartime personalities still active, such as Stalin until 1953 or Eisenhower who was President of the United States 1953–61 (and who outlived him).

Consequently many historians went on to make a reputation through iconoclasm, and no one was a greater iconic hero to rail against than Winston Churchill. On the left, his activities against trade unionists, and on the right, the fall of the British Empire became benchmarks against which to find Churchill wanting. In particular Alan Clark – later a maverick right-wing Conservative MP – along with those of a similar ilk in the United States, made what to many was the morally outrageous claim that Britain should have done a deal with Hitler in 1940. This would, in the eyes of its protagonists, have allowed the British Empire to survive – it was the decision to continue the war that bankrupted Britain and ceded superpower status to the United States.

This view, plus the attempt by many of the iconoclasts to restore what they felt to be the unfairly sullied reputation of Neville Chamberlain and the virtues of appeasement, proved too much for most people. In addition, many historians felt that this approach was to view Churchill through the lens of contemporary debate rather than to see him in the context of his own time. Added to this, the end of the Cold War and

the defeat of Soviet Communism completely changed the way in which historians viewed the Bolshevik era of 1917–91. Consequently, after the Churchillian *thesis*, and the revisionist *antithesis*, came what one might describe as a more measured and nuanced approach to his life.

Certainly Churchill made mistakes: Gallipoli, returning Britain to the gold standard in 1925, opposing Indian self-rule. He was a man of his own era. But compared to the heroic decision he made in 1940 to resist Hitler and preserve freedom, all his blemishes pale into such comparative insignificance that his overall heroic status is restored. Of course he wrote history to his own advantage, but who

does not? In seeing the future of the Great Republic – the United States – as he did, he was surely entirely correct? And his support of science and innovation was not only war-winning but ahead of its time. History will therefore be kind to Churchill, even if it is no longer he who writes it.

ABOVE: The landmark statue of Sir Winston Churchill in Parliament Square in London – now arguably one of the capital's most famous sites.

Index

Credits

The publishers would like to thank the following sources for their kind permission to reproduce the pictures in this book.

Key: t = top, b = bottom, c = centre and r = right and l = left

4-5. Fox Photos/Hulton Archive/Getty Images, 6. Betmman/Getty, 8. Arte & Immagini srl/CORBIS/Corbis via Getty, 9. Mirrorpix, 10-11. Bridgeman Images/National Army Museum, London/Acquired with assistance of National Art Collections Fund, The Battle of Blenheim on the 13th August 1704, c.1743 (oil on canvas), 13t. Mirrorpix, 13bl. Bridgeman Images/Private Collection, Sir Winston Churchill, aged four years old, 1878 (oil on canvas), Ayron Ward, P. (19th century), 13br. Bridgeman Images/The Churchill Collection National Trust Photographic Library/Derrick E. Witty, Lord Randolph Churchill (oil on canvas), English School, (19th century), 14l. Getty Images, 14r. Mirrorpix, 15. Churchill Archives Centre, The Churchill Papers, CHAR 28/44/7, 16-17. Mirrorpix, 18. The Bridgeman Art Library/National Army Museum, London, Charge of the 21st Lancers at the Battle of Omdurman on 2nd September 1898, 1899 (oil on canvas), 19. Churchill Archives Centre, The Churchill Papers, CHAR 28/114/3, 20. Getty Images/Time & Life Pictures, 21. Bridgeman Images/Private Collection/Ken Welsh, Wanted poster for escaped prisoner of war Churchill, from 'A Roving Commission by Winston S. Churchill', published by Scribner's, 1930 (litho), South African School, (19th century), 24l. Mirrorpix, 24r-25. Getty Images, 26. Getty Images, 27. Churchill Archives Centre, The Churchill Papers, CHAR 4/8/117, 28. Bridgeman Images/The Churchill Collection National Trust Photographic Library/Derrick E. Witty, Portrait of Winston Churchill, 1916 (oil on canvas), Lavery, Sir John (1856-1941)/Chartwell, Kent, UK, 30. Mirrorpix, 31. George Rinhart/Corbis via Getty Images, 32. (CB) Churchill Archives Centre, The Churchill Papers CHAR 13/57/3, 33-34. Mirrorpix, 35. Getty Images, 36. Mirrorpix, 37. Getty Images, 38-39. Churchill Archives Centre, The papers of Clementine Ogilvy Spencer-Churchill, Baroness Spencer-Churchill of Chartwell CSCT 2/8/2-3, 40. Mirrorpix, 41. Getty Images, 42-43. Churchill Archives Centre, The papers of Clementine Ogilvy Spencer-Churchill, Baroness Spencer-Churchill of Chartwell CSCT 2/8/6, 44. Getty Images, 46-47. Mirrorpix, 48. Bridgeman Images/Roy Miles Fine Paintings, Riveria Scene, 1930's (oil on canvas), Sir Winston Churchill (1874-1965) 49. Bridgeman Images/The Churchill Collection National Trust Photographic Library/Derrick E. Witty, Gate at Marrakech, Man on Donkey (oil on canvas), Sir Winston Churchill(1874-1965), Chartwell, Kent, UK, 50-53. Mirrorpix, 54. Private Collection, 55t. Getty Images, 55b. Getty Images, 56. Bridgeman Images/Archives du Ministere des Affaires Etrangeres, Paris, France/Archives Charmet, Map of 1910 showing the Sykes-Picot Agreement of 1916 (coloured engraving), English School, (20th century), 57-59. Getty Images, 60-61t. Mirrorpix, 61b Topfoto, 62-63. Getty Images, 64. Mirrorpix, 65t. Getty Images, 65b. Bridgeman Images/Private Collection, Chartwell House (oil on canvas), Sir Winston Churchill (1874-1965), 66. Getty Images/Time & Life Pictures, 67. Getty Images/Popperfoto, 68-69. Churchill Archives Centre, The Churchill Papers, CHAR 1/201/65a, 70. Mirrorpix, 71-73. Getty Images, 74-75. Getty Images/Popperfoto, 76bl. Mirrorpix, 76br. Getty Images, 77. Getty Images/New York Daily News Archive, 78. Mary Evans Picture Library, 79. Hulton-Deutsch Collection/CORBIS/Corbis via Getty Images, 80. Getty Images, 81. Keystone-France/Gamma-Keystone via Getty Images, 82-83. Getty Images, 84-85. Churchill Archives Centre, The papers of Clementine Ogilvy Spencer-Churchill, Baroness Spencer-Churchill of Chartwell, CSCT 1/1/12, 86-87. Churchill Archives Centre, The papers of Clementine Ogilvy Spencer-Churchill, Baroness Spencer-Churchill of Chartwell CSCT 2/2/25, 88. Getty Images/Time & Life Pictures, 90. Mirrorpix, 91-93. Getty Images, 94t. Getty Images/Popperfoto, 94b, Topfoto, 95. Churchill Archives Centre, The Churchill Papers CHAR 20/85/61, 96-97 PA Images, 98. Getty Images/Time & Life Pictures, 99. Getty Images, 100c. Peter Macdiarmid/Getty Images, 100b. CPT TANNER - No 2 Army Film and /AFP/Getty Images, 101t. Pol Roger Ltd, 101b. Mirrorpix, 102t & 102b. Imperial War Museums, London (E 1579 & E 3282), 103. Mirrorpix, 104l. U.S. National Archives and Records Administration, Washington, 104r PA Images, 105. U.S. National Archives and Records Administration, Washington, 106. Getty Images, 107. Churchill Archives Centre, The Churchill Papers CHAR 20/85/61, 108-109. Getty Images, 110-111. Churchill Archives Centre, The Churchill Papers CHAR 20/52/28-29, 112. Mirrorpix, 113t. Getty Images,113b & 114-115. Imperial War Museums, London (E 18971 & A 12649), 116. Getty Images, 117-118. Mirrorpix, 119-121. Getty Images, 122. Mirrorpix, 123. Getty Images, 124-126t. Mirrorpix, 126. PA Images, 127-130t. Getty Images, 130-131b. Mirrorpix, 132. Churchill Archives Centre, The Churchill Papers CHAR 1/104b/66, 133t. Mirrorpix, 133b. Getty Images, 134-137. Getty Images, 138l. Mirrorpix, 138r. Popperfoto/Getty Images, 139. Churchill Archives Centre, The Churchill Papers CHAR 2/230B/350, 140. Getty Images/Time & Life Pictures, 141. Churchill Archives Centre, Other Deposited Collections relating to Sir Winston Churchill, WCHL 16/5/4, 142tl & 142tr. Mirrorpix, 142b Getty Images, 143. Churchill Archives Centre, The Churchill Papers CHUR 1/94/165, 144-149. Getty Images, 150. PA Images, 151t. Getty Images, 151b. Alamy/Neil Grant, 152-153. Mirrorpix, 154-155, Getty Images, 157. Alamy/Neil Grant,

pages 15, 19, 27, 68-69, 110-111, 132, 140 Reproduced with permission of the Churchill Archives Centre, Cambridge College, Cambridge.

pages 32, 38-39, 42-43, 86-87, 95, 107 Reproduced with permission of Curtis Brown Ltd, London on behalf of The Estate of Sir Winston Churchill.

page 84-85 Reproduced with permission of the Master, Fellows and Scholars of Churchill College, Cambridge, Copyright © Clementine Churchill

page 139 Reproduced with permission of The National Churchill Museum, Fulton Missouri

page 143 Reproduced with permission of Lester Piggot

Every effort has been made to acknowledge correctly and contact the source and/or copyright holder of each picture and Carlton Books Limited apologises for any unintentional errors or omissions, which will be corrected in future editions of this book.